Manager's Guide to Navigating Change

Other titles in the Briefcase Books series include:

To learn more about titles in the Briefcase Books series go to
www.briefcasebooks.com

Manager's Guide to Navigating Change

Stephen Rock

McGraw-Hill

New York Chicago San Francisco Lisbon
London Madrid Mexico City Milan New Delhi
San Juan Seoul Singapore Sydney Toronto

1 2 3 4 5 6 7 8 9 0 QFR/QFR 1 8 7 6 5 4 3 2

ISBN   978-0-07-176947-1
MHID   0-07-176947-1

e-ISBN   978-0-07-177614-1
e-MHID   0-07-177614-1

This is a CWL Publishing Enterprises book developed for McGraw-Hill by CWL Publishing Enterprises, Inc., Madison, Wisconsin, www.cwlpub.com.

Product or brand names used in this book may be trade names or trademarks. Where we believe there may be proprietary claims to such trade names or trademarks, the name has been used with an initial capital or it has been capitalized in the style used by the name claimant. Regardless of the capitalization used, all such names have been used in an editorial manner without any intent to convey endorsement of or other affiliation with the name claimant. Neither the author nor the publisher intends to express any judgment as to the validity or legal status of any such proprietary claims.

McGraw-Hill books are available at special quantity discounts to use as premiums and sales promotions, or for use in corporate training programs. To contact a representative, please e-mail us at bulksales@mcgraw-hill.com.

This book is printed on acid-free paper.

Contents

Acknowledgments

Writing is a collaborative effort, and there were many who contributed to the development of this book. Sue Reynard and Jocelyn Godfrey were able to find words when I couldn't. My sister, Lesley Rock, was clearly able to best her older brother when it came to editing. A former colleague, Lorraine Cregar, was instrumental in teaching me many communication concepts and encouraged me to document our company's discoveries. Finally, John Woods of CWL Publishing Enterprises, who recruited me to write this book, found the patience he never knew he had. Thank you to all.

There are also quite a few clients whose collaboration and support enabled many of my unique concepts to move from ideas to tried and tested approaches. Thank you to Dan Gundlach, Paul Marabella, Bill Downs, Angela Mangiapane, Juergen Zirnstein, Leanne Metz, Vern McCrory, and John Spicer.

Finally, I extend my greatest thanks to my family. You'll read quite a few stories about Melissa, Merideth, Samantha, and Caroline Rock. If I wasn't trying to change them, they were trying to change me. Thank you for your patience, support, and love.

Introduction

One of my earliest memories is telling my parents that I saw a policeman getting out of a taxicab in our neighborhood. It turned out he was a military officer returning home from Vietnam.

- A few months ago, I made a Skype call, via a mobile phone Internet service, from the backseat of a Mercedes–Benz in Ho Chi Minh City, Vietnam. Nothing about that call was even remotely conceivable during my youth.
- A more recent memory is watching the Tiananmen Square demonstrations on CNN in 1989. Students were protesting for economic and political reform. Not long after, my wife gave birth to our first child.
- Fast-forward 20 years to today. My daughter speaks fluent Mandarin Chinese and recently spent a semester studying at the University of Beijing, which is not far from Tiananmen Square—a place of tranquility.

A lot has changed—not only world affairs but also how the world communicates and operates.

I write these words while sitting in a Starbucks—also in China. Across the busy street is an IKEA. The woman next to me has a shopping bag from H&M—a department store with 2,600 stores in 44 markets—and is speaking on an iPhone. I'm working on a project for an American-based company whose business presence in China will soon be larger than it is in the United States And, I will probably be eating my dinner at KFC or Pizza Hut tonight.

The pace of how business—and life—is conducted is getting faster and faster. Sure, I can wonder how my U.S.-born baby grew so quickly into a Chinese-speaking young woman, but it is far more staggering to think about how the world's politics, technology, and economics have changed in the past 20 years.

The executives of your company are looking at this pace of change and trying to stay one step ahead. Or if they aren't trying to stay ahead, they are desperately trying to catch up. It is only a matter of time before large-scale change impacts where you work. There's no denying the truism that *change is constant*. Competing in an ever-accelerating world creates an imperative for organizations: *The only way to win in the marketplace is to be able to adapt quickly.*

The following are just a few change strategy examples implemented by companies that adapted appropriately to shifts in the marketplace:

- **Adjusting to radically different cost structures** (based on new delivery models). A $1 billion company that manufactures products for the automotive industry saw its business come to an abrupt halt as the economy struggled in 2008. It literally had no demand. When demand returned, the company had gained new competitors from Asia, selling products at a price point lower than the American company's cost of manufacturing. To survive, the company needed to simultaneously cut costs from an already lean organization, figure out how to add services to justify a higher price point, increase the quality of its products, and reinvent its entire supply chain. It also had to replace its entire information technology infrastructure. Added to these challenges was a very unmotivated workforce.

- **Adjusting to permanently different energy costs.** A company produced a rather heavy product in a few highly efficient factories and trucked the finished product throughout the country. When energy costs increased dramatically, an analysis showed that the company would be better off having more factories—even less efficient factories—distributed around the country. This configuration would dramatically cut trucking costs and distances. The company had to change its entire supply chain configuration. What was once a manufacturing efficiency advantage had become a distribution cost liability. Old factories would need to close and new factories would need to open. Although delivering the exact same product, the company needed to look completely different.

- **Adapting to global demographics and market shifts.** A baby products company faced a similar need for major change. The U.S. market was not growing, so the company needed to move into emerging economies and add children's products to its portfolio. To make such sweeping changes successful, the company needed to build new systems; add new competencies to its R&D, marketing, and customer service operations; and develop new skill sets. In the quarter-to-quarter world of investor expectations, it wouldn't fly to say that this was a 10-year effort. The company had to demonstrate rapid progress every year.

- **Taking advantage of Internet/Web capabilities.** A retailer that repaired small appliances found itself in the position where not enough local customers were repairing their appliances to make the business viable. It was easier for most customers to throw out their appliances and buy new ones. On a national basis, however, plenty of business still existed. So the retailer, which just a few years ago couldn't even spell the word *Internet*, opened a Web-based distribution business. Within three years, the former retail-only business became the leading distributor and Web-retailer for replacement parts in its industry. The tired, old brick-and-mortar retail location closed, and a new warehouse opened. The most valuable employee was no longer the person who could repair the appliance; it was the person, often from the younger generation, who excelled at Internet marketing.

Do you recognize how these trends may impact your workplace? Are your managers, owners, or customers expecting you to do something to adjust to these trends—right now?

Companies still need to continuously deal with incremental changes—the gradual evolution of product lines, services, organizational structures and policies, and so on. But in this age of hyperspeed, I'm seeing more and more companies trying to leapfrog over past performances to achieve transformational change (the kind where the future state is suddenly quite different from the past).

So the question becomes, does your organization need a formal management program? The answer is, you do need one if you're undergoing any of the following:

- Outsourcing
- Major system implementation
- Repositioning
- Reorganization
- Integration following an acquisition or merger
- Culture changes/leadership turnover
- Facility changes

Although the world is changing at hyperspeed, it doesn't mean you can take shortcuts in your effort to go quickly. Every company has to manage change, and doing it *well* has never been more important. Being able to change quickly and effectively may make the difference between whether your company suffers, survives, or thrives in this new age. This book shows you how to achieve sustainable, effective change in an organization, and how to do it efficiently.

Content Highlights

You can journey through these pages cover-to-cover, or you can skip around, dipping into individual chapters for answers to your most pressing questions. Here's a quick review of what the chapters cover.

Chapter 1 discusses the business case for organizational change management. Change management isn't just consultant mumbo-jumbo. Putting your company's resources into a change initiative delivers returns far greater than the cost of the initial effort.

Chapter 2 discusses how organizational change starts with personal change. Getting a group of people to change the way they think requires understanding how individuals process change.

Chapter 3 returns to the concepts of organizational change and encourages you to focus on your end goal or vision.

Chapter 4 discusses how you can ensure that your change program is effective. Sustainable change requires comprehensive alignment of objectives, work methods, and people. This chapter is a detailed discussion of how an organization works, how people are organized to do work, and how enablers support that work.

Chapter 5 lays out an approach to structuring your change initiative, and Chapters 6–10 discuss the five key strategies of any change management initiative: awareness, understanding, participation, leverage, and measurement.

Chapter 11 discusses how you can keep everybody working on the right things with an effective governance structure.

Finally, Chapter 12 brings it all together with some tough lessons that I have learned and words of encouragement for you as you lead your peers through change.

Special Features

The idea behind the books in the Briefcase Series is to give you practical information written in a friendly person-to-person style. The chapters are relatively short, deal with tactical issues, and include lots of examples. They also feature numerous boxes designed to give you different types of specific information. Here's a description of the boxes you'll find in this book:

KEY TERM Every subject has some jargon, including this one, dealing with change management. These sidebars provide definitions of terms and concepts as they are introduced.

SMART MANAGING These sidebars do just what their name suggests: give you tips to intelligently apply the strategies and tactics described here to reduce costs, improve productivity, and create a positive change environment for all employees.

TRICKS OF THE TRADE Tricks of the Trade sidebars give you insider how-to hints on techniques astute managers use to execute the tactics described in this book.

It's always useful to have examples that show how the principles in the book are applied. These sidebars provide descriptions of case studies where effective change management improved results.

Caution sidebars provide warnings for where things could go wrong when undergoing change so you can anticipate and make sure things go well.

How can you make sure you won't make a mistake when you're trying to implement the techniques the book describes? You can't, but these sidebars give you practical advice on how to minimize the possibility of things going wrong.

This icon identifies sidebars where you'll find specific procedures, techniques, or technology you can use to successfully implement the book's principles and practices.

Manager's Guide
to Navigating Change

Chapter
1

Faster, Easier Changes: The Business Case for Change Management

It is not the strongest of the species that survives, nor the most intelligent, but rather the one most adaptable to change.
—Commonly misattributed to Charles Darwin

Chances are excellent that if you are reading this book you have already experienced a "bad" change experience—perhaps something akin to one of the following situations:

The Consultant Rumor. One day, a consultant team arrives and begins asking questions. You're told they're here to "identify operational efficiency opportunities." You and your peers begin to compare notes on the questions being asked. Senior management isn't providing clear answers.

One of my earliest work experiences was with a project called C 90. It was rumored that this project was designed to cut costs to 90 percent of current levels. One employee had heard of a project called C 90 in another company that was doing exactly the same thing. Communication from senior management was so poor that there was nothing in writing on the project. The biggest surprise was that the project was actually called See 90. It was about identifying key areas that the company should focus on in 1990. Total costs weren't going to be cut.

The Surprise. Four days before Christmas, the company announces that it is offering a voluntary separation package to many people. If the company does not receive enough voluntary acceptances, involuntary cuts will begin as soon as March. People are given eight days to decide to accept the offer. People are shocked because the company was just finishing a fantastic year.

What nobody had communicated was that the company was preparing for a large increase in raw material costs. Management offered the voluntary program at year-end so the company could pay for it with the great earnings of the current year rather than the expected poor earnings from the upcoming year. Nobody had a good holiday season.

The Ill-Conceived. A company made an acquisition, and as part of the acquisition, it decided to consolidate operations in another city. This surprising news was shared with all employees on a Monday morning. "Many of you will be given the opportunity to move, but this facility will be closing." Certainly this news was a surprise, and the situation was one that could not be avoided.

The ill-conceived side of this announcement was that there was a second business unit colocated in the facility that was to be closed. Nobody had bothered to think about what would happen to the second business unit if the first one were to close. Nobody in the second unit had even been told of the acquisition. The general manager of the second business unit found out at the same time as everybody else in the building.

The Killer Information Technology Project. The IT group works for months with a small group of users to design new processes to roll out with a new system. They have an inspiring project name and a newsletter that comes out regularly.

The project starts to slip, however, and the training schedule gets shortened. Much of what is taught in training becomes "how to perform a transaction" in the system. There isn't time to explain the overall process and when the transaction is to be used. When the launch, or go-live, occurs, in theory people could press the right buttons to do work in the new way—but no one's been told why and how to! Mistakes and frustration mount. Customer orders aren't being shipped. Vendors aren't getting paid. Even worse, employees aren't being reimbursed for travel expenses. Credit cards are being shut off by the card provider. Productivity completely disappears.

The variations on the "bad change" stories are endless. I like them because they help me make the case that change management is not only a little tinder you throw onto a project. Change management is the fuel that makes a project successful, and doing it well requires planning, resources, and execution.

Changing the "Change Curve"

Think about any major change that you've personally gone through. How much time did it steal from you being able to get your "real work" done? Think not only about the time you had to spend learning what was going on and getting trained in new policies, procedures, or equipment—but also the time you were distracted by gossip, fears about the future, and concerns for yourself and your coworkers.

> **Organizational Change Management (OCM)** A structured approach for moving a group of people **KEY TERM** from one state to a significantly different state. OCM's goal is to reduce the disorder typically associated with periods of change and help people resume their pre-change levels of productivity as quickly as possible. Well-run change management efforts empower those affected by the change, giving them a voice in how the change progresses so they more easily accept and engage in the desired, future state.

Now add to that the impact on every other employee affected by the change: the time they spend learning about and coping with the change they can't spend on their "real work." No wonder that productivity invariably drops when a change is introduced (Figure 1-1).

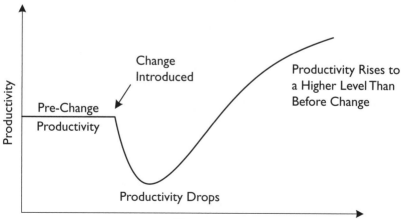

Figure 1-1. Impact of change

When a change is introduced, people must spend time learning what is going to change, developing new skills, installing new technology, defining new processes, and so on. Plus there is usually a lot of mental energy that goes into worry about the future. That's why productivity always drops immediately after a change is introduced before it begins to rise. The hope is that the change will lead to an even higher level of productivity as people eventually grow comfortable with and competent in the new methods.

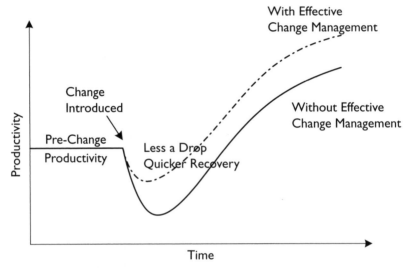

Figure 1-2. Goal of change management

The goal of change management is to shift this impact curve—lessen the drop in productivity, raise productivity faster, and achieve an even better outcome (see Figure 1-2).

It surprises me that so many companies give change management short shrift. They tend to muddle through their change efforts, barely communicating and thinking that people will soon come around. What this "cross our fingers and hope" approach ignores is the significant economic opportunity cost that is introduced by the turmoil of transformational change.

To illustrate this point, think about this hypothetical scenario. Let's say 1,000 employees, each of whom costs an average of $80,000 per year, work in a business that generates $330 million in revenue per year. The

	Base Case
Total Revenue	$330,000,000
Employees	1,000
Revenue/Employee	$330,000
Cost/Employee	$80,000
Value Creation/Employee/Year	$250,000
Value Creation/Employee/Month	$20,833
Productivity During Change Period	90%
Missing Productivity	10%
Value of Missing Productivity/Month	$2,083
Months of Change Initiative	12
Initiative Opportunity Cost	$25,000,000

Table 1-1. Value created by each employee

cost of labor in this organization is $80 million. We can conclude that the value created by each employee is $250,000 per year (see Table 1-1).

During a change effort, you know you're losing some percentage of their time. For the purpose here, let's assume that they are only 90 percent productive during this period. This means a 10 percent loss. Over the course of a 12-month initiative, you would forgo the creation of $25M in value for your company.

Before you reject the underlying concept here, note that the forgone value may not be easily seen. Sure, it's easy to see the loss of value when costs increase because employees have to go to training. But think of the hidden costs. What about a research scientist who is worried about losing his or her job in a reorganization? As a result of not working as hard, the scientist develops something several months later than he or she might have.

Opportunity costs The value you miss out on by investing in something else. Had Apple decided to go into high-end computer servers instead of iPhones, the opportunity costs would have been very high because it would have missed out on all the iPhone revenues. Every management decision has opportunity costs.

KEY TERM

Think about the salespeople who are gossiping about the change program instead of calling on customers. The value disappears like heat leaving a drafty house. You know it's leaving, but you will never find all the cracks.

Suppose you could shorten the time frame (see the "faster" column in Table 1-2) or have less of a drop, say only 5 percent (the "better" column), or, ideally, both. You can avoid millions of dollars in opportunity costs. In this scenario, being able to do a change just 1/12th faster and by cutting the productivity loss to 5 percent, this organization would capture $13.5 million in opportunity costs.

	Base Case	Better	Faster	Both
Total Revenue	$330,000,000			
Employees	1,000			
Revenue/Employee	$330,000			
Cost/Employee	$80,000			
Value Creation/Employee/Year	$250,000			
Value Creation/Employee/Month	$20,833			
Productivity During Change Period	90%	95%	90%	95%
Missing Productivity	10%	5%	10%	5%
Value of Missing Productivity/Month	$2,083	$1,042	$2,083	$1,042
Months of Change Initiative	12	12	11	11
Initiative Opportunity Cost	$25,000,000	$12,500,000	$22,916,667	$11,458,333
Value Recaptured Through Change Management		$12,500,000	$2,083,333	$13,541,667

Table 1-2. The value of of improvement

Even if the numbers for your company differ from this scenario, the concept is the same: effective change management enables your organization to avoid missed opportunities to create value, and it does so by increasing productivity and quickening the pace of change.

Change Management Isn't Rocket Science

For a lot of people, hearing that they've just been assigned to lead a change in their area of responsibility is considered bad news—likely because they've had some of the bad change experiences described earlier.

And now you've just been asked to play a major role in a change

---

> ## CHANGE MANAGEMENT NEEDS A NEW NAME
>
> **CAUTION**
>
> There is a crying need for change within the change management field. It needs a new name. There are two fields of change management. In the information technology world, change management is all about the practice of methodically changing pieces of technology. If you used it to change a flat tire, change management would ensure you put all the lug nuts on the new tire.
>
> Organizational change management isn't about controlling changes—or even managing them. Organizational change management is about the *process* of leading people through change and helping them reach a new state as quickly and as easily as possible.

effort, perhaps even lead it. You've been told, "This is a great career opportunity for you if you succeed." Having lived through poorly managed change efforts, you are well aware of what it means to fail.

A mentor suggests your best bet is change management. "Great," you think. "Another complicated, mumbo-jumbo program thought up by consultants. Worse, it could be something thought up by the folks in human resources or corporate communications." You research the topic and find a description something like "A structured approach to move people from a current state to a future state in an effective and efficient manner." Your day has gone from bad to worse.

But there is good news. Change management isn't rocket science. Change management is a combination of three things: *strong leadership, good planning*, and an *investment of time*.

In fact, change management is so easy that I bet you're already using it at home.

Almost Everybody Uses Change Management at Home

Yes, you really do use change management at home. Let's look at a "major change" in a family and discuss what would likely happen. Suppose, for example, that you've decided you want your family to live a healthier lifestyle.

One option is to simply impose these changes on your family. Change your grocery shopping list, stop the take-out trips, force the spouse and children on hikes or bike rides every day. I bet you know exactly what you'd get from this approach: a lot of resentful, rebellious people living in

---

SKILLS OF A NON-ROCKET SCIENTIST

SMART

MANAGING

Though change management isn't rocket science, specific skills are needed to be good at the job. You will be more effective as a change manager if you:

- Can always maintain a positive attitude and can fully support your management's plans
- Know how people go through significant change and genuinely want to help people as they experience change
- Are able to influence people to act
- Have exceptional written and verbal communication skills
- Can keep confidential information confidential
- Have the confidence of management and the trust of the organization
- Can be more than a manager, supervisor, or team member: *be a leader*

---

your house! Children snacking behind your back, a spouse who stops off for a burger before coming home from work, people who disappear at the "exercise hour." With a lot of yelling and nagging, you may ultimately see some change, but it will be a hard slog with questionable results.

No, if you were serious about the change, imposition would not be the way to go about it.

If you were serious, you'd have to be more thoughtful and deliberate in how you approach this change.

- You'd have a clear *vision* for your change, in this case, a healthier family.
- You might read up on nutritional and exercise guidelines so you'd have a basis for making decisions. You'd think about your food budget and whether you could afford new exercise or sports equipment, or fees if a family member wants to join an organized sport team. (Let's call this the *scope of effort*.)
- You'd want to shape a *framework* that will help you deal with all your family members so they embrace the effort.
- You'd want to educate them (in an age-appropriate way if you have children).
- You'd want to work with your spouse so you're in full agreement on how to make the changes. For example, you could replace food rewards with other activities, such as playing miniature golf.

■ You'd want to get your spouse and children involved in preparation of healthy meals.

■ Before talking about the changes with the full family, you'd want to have specific plans in place for the *execution*: actions you will start taking immediately to implement the changes.

Change Management in a Business Context

Once you understand these basic components, it's easy to translate them into a business context (Table 1-3).

Component	Organizational Change Management
Vision What does the future look like?	Where does management want to take the organization, what is management's definition of success, and how will you know when you have achieved success?
Scope In what areas will you apply efforts?	How will you ensure that your organization's objectives, business process, and human resources are in alignment and appropriately reflect the desired change?
Framework How will you approach the effort?	What process will you follow to ensure the work is done completely and sequenced appropriately? In later chapters we will cover the ASPIRE Model for organizing the work that must get done. ■ Assess the as-is ■ Set standards ■ Plan programs ■ Implement initiatives ■ Recognize results ■ Evaluate effectiveness
Execution The steps for implementing the change	What macro-level approaches will you use to foster the desired change? ■ Awareness ■ Understanding ■ Engagement ■ Leverage ■ Measurement

Table 1-3. Pillars of change management

I expect that some of the terms in this table (such as the ASPIRE Model) are new to you. Don't worry. The core of this book is structured around these components:

- Vision: Chapter 3
- Scope: Chapter 4
- Framework: Chapter 5
- Execution: Chapters 6 to 10

There is a brief detour in Chapter 2, where I talk about some basics of how people react to change that you will need to keep in mind as you plan and execute the change. Plus there are two final chapters that address broader issues around implementing a change management plan.

What Does and Doesn't Affect Change Management

This book is designed to give you a road map through the change process. As your guidebook, it is meant to cut years off your learning curve. Right up front, however, you should know the following:

The nature of change does not vary based on industry. I have seen change in places as varied as a candy company, an iron foundry, an insurance service provider, a telecommunications company, and a global accounting firm. In the end, people drive change, not industries.

National cultures, however, create variability in the way change is managed. One approach might work in the United States, Canada, Australia, and the UK. The same approach definitely will not work in Germany, China, or France. How people typically interact with their leaders has more to do with how to manage change in their environment than industry classifications do.

Workforce dynamics play a huge role in managing change. People act differently in an Internet start-up versus a governmental agency versus a unionized heavy manufacturer versus a professional services organization in a right-to-work state. A successful organization is frequently harder to change than a failing organization.

The tactics you would use in a large organization are unworkable in a small organization. Layers of cascading messages would be appropriate in the larger organization, where a smaller organization could just gather people in the cafeteria. That said, the leader needs to communicate to everyone throughout the course of the project.

Change Management Works

If you thought it was good news that change management is not rocket science, I have even better news for you: it works. Executing an effective change management program does two critically important things:

1. It enables your organization to reach its goals more quickly and with greater productivity than it would under any other circumstances ("shifting the curve," as I talked about earlier in the chapter).
2. It enables you to exhibit the kinds of skills that top leaders need to have. Top leaders know how to place their people first—and relish the opportunity to rest comfortably when the job is done well.

By paying attention to change management, you will not only help your company achieve a transition more quickly and smoothly, but you'll learn valuable leadership skills. It's a win-win situation for all involved. Remember, senior management expects you to deliver.

CHANGE MANAGEMENT CAN BE USED OUTSIDE THE BUSINESS ENVIRONMENT AS WELL

FOR EXAMPLE

I don't often mix business with religion, but as it happens, my church recently named a new pastor. Our previous leader was very focused on education, and classes abounded. Our new pastor has different priorities. The church isn't a business, but it is an organization, and this new leader has embarked on a change. He needs to apply change leadership concepts in a nonbusiness environment.

To help the organization understand and be engaged in this new direction, he is using a variety of techniques from the business world. There are one-way communications, two-way dialogue sessions, and small groups to engage in building the new approach for the church. The new pastor is focused on working with those people who lead committees, and he is also focused on measuring our progress.

Some people, still living with the voice of the previous pastor in their head, have responded, "We should have a class on how to do this well." The new pastor is remaining steadfast in his principles and leadership plan. He is making change management work in a nonbusiness environment.

Manager's Checklist for Chapter 1

☑ Change management is not extra seasoning thrown onto a project. It is the main ingredient that determines success.

☑ Effective change management requires planning, resources, and execution.

☑ The goal of change management is to alter the "change curve" by lessening the inevitable productivity drop and speeding up the achievement of higher performance levels than were previously seen.

☑ Change management isn't rocket science. Most of us use the basic components in our daily lives. What it requires is strong leadership, good planning, and an investment of time.

☑ The nature of change is the same across industries, but it can be affected by national cultures, social norms, and so on.

Organizational Change Starts with Individual Change

When the winds of change are blowing, some people are building shelters; others are building windmills.

—Ancient Chinese Proverb

People of all walks have been dealing with change for at least as long as there has been a written record. One of the oldest Chinese texts is the *I Ching*, or *Yi Jing*, which literally translates as *Classic of Changes*. Dating back to at least the third century BC, the *Yi Jing* is a means of gaining insight into a question using a standardized process of throwing coins and interpreting the results in one of 64 ways.

Although one might place a low value on the random nature of insight that was gained, the ancient Chinese had perhaps a better understanding of change than we do today. The Chinese character *Yi* refers to three aspects of change. First is that nature provides us with ongoing change. Births and deaths happen, the tides come and go, seasons change, and the sun rises and sets. Second is that change follows rules. As an example, as the days become short, the weather grows colder. We can always count on the sun rising in the east and setting in the west. Third is that change becomes easy when one is able to see and understand that which is constant and that which is changing.

Sounds great: Change follows certain rules. Once you understand the nature of the change and that which remains constant, it will all be easy, and you will feel peaceful.

This may sound like an alien way of thinking, but you can easily see it on a personal level. Think about a movie in which a character has to explain to a child some form of major change. The dialogue would run along the following lines: "Jimmy ... Mommy and Daddy love you very much, and we love being a family. We love being a family so much we decided that we would like to make the family bigger, and Mommy is going to have another baby. You will have a brother or sister. You will always be our oldest child, and we will always love you with all our heart, but we will soon be a larger family." The father has explained to the child that change will occur, what the change is, and what will not change.

The concepts are the same in business. Think about an organizational change you've gone through. I'm sure you can think of an example when the change didn't go well. What was your biggest complaint? For many, the answer is "I was completely stressed out. I didn't know what was going on." You were stressed out because you didn't know what was going to change, how it would affect you, and what was going to stay the same. You also didn't know the rules or principles that were being used to govern the change.

SMART MANAGING

COMMUNICATE THE RIGHT THINGS

Let's be realistic. Many executives only want to communicate when all the decisions are final. They believe that communicating before all the decisions are made will create unneeded stress in the organization. They don't want to have to eat their words. "They won't be able to do anything, so why bother telling them?"

Unfortunately, it's impossible to not communicate. Keeping quiet may buy short-term peace, but it jeopardizes the leader's long-term credibility among those he or she leads. Instead of not communicating (which only leads to speculation) or communicating only when decisions have already been made, you should communicate two things. (1) Describe the criteria by which you will make your decisions. (2) Explain when you will make the decision. If you follow through on those two points, everybody who is impacted will say that they were treated fairly and respectfully. In the spirit of intelligent leadership, people will trust your decisions. In the spirit of Yi Jing, you have given them the rules by which they can understand the change, and that understanding will prevent personal and organizational turmoil.

The Biology and Psychology of Change

Think for a moment about your high school biology class. Remember the term homeostasis? *Homeostasis* is the process by which an organism self-regulates its internal environment so that it maintains stability. For example, a single-cell organism might regulate its temperature or pH levels.

Now think about humans. It's a leap from a single-cell organism to the complexity of a human being, but homeostasis is an important part of our biological functioning, as well. My brother-in-law comes north to visit from Florida, and he is always cold on very nice days. When I travel south to visit him, I am always hot on days he calls nice. At a biological level, this is an example of our bodies dealing with unexpected change.

I'm sure scientists could explain the impact of such change on our bodies, but it's not something we have a lot of direct control over. What's easier to influence is our thought process.

Let me describe the thoughts that were occurring at a client of mine. This company had been extraordinarily successful for many years, but the 2008 recession hit it hard. The industry was going through a shakeout, and many of its competitors were declaring bankruptcy. In the first months of a project, most middle managers would say things like, "We've gone through down cycles before. The things we did in the past made us successful in the past, and there is no reason to change."

As time progressed and business did not improve, the common refrain was "How did management let this happen?! I made commitments based on a bonus I'm not going to get. It is their fault, and I'm the one paying the price." Soon, those thoughts moved to a combination of depression and willingness to try new things. "It doesn't matter what we do. Until our customers fix their problems, we'll continue to be in trouble."

After that, it took six to nine months before most people were engaged in trying to change the way the organization operated. The interesting part of this situation was that it was all fairly predictable with a little understanding of human psychology.

While I don't believe managers have to become psychologists to effectively lead change, it does help to know how humans react to change. Perhaps the best-known model of reaction to change is Elisabeth Kübler-Ross's *Five Stages of Grief*, introduced in 1969. Kübler-Ross formulated this model based on how dying patients dealt with their impending death, but in the past 40 years, we've come to see that it portrays how people cope with any major change. Here's a quick recap of the stages, adapted as they relate to organizational change:

Denial. "Nothing is wrong." "Nothing can happen to me." In this stage, people act as if nothing has changed. Early anxiety may lead them to pay particular attention to what they like about their life as it exists today (job responsibilities, coworkers, comfort, feeling skillful).

Anger. "Why me?" "This isn't fair!" "Whose fault is it?" In this stage, people realize that they can no longer deny something is happening. They become angry that the change is being forced on them and look around for someone to blame.

Bargaining. "What can I do to stop this?" "I'll do anything I can so I can make things like they were before." The third stage involves the hope that the individual can stop or even reverse the impeding change.

Depression. "It's hopeless." "What's the point in trying anymore?" During the fourth stage, people begin to understand the certainty of the change. If they're closely tied to the old way of working, they start mourning the impending loss.

Acceptance. "Well, maybe everything will be OK." "Maybe there is a chance this will work for me." In this last stage, the individual begins to come to terms with the change.

The stages of grief map fairly closely to the change curve introduced in Figure 1-1, Chapter 1. Productivity begins to fall when employees go through denial and choose not to accept that change must occur or has begun to occur. They talk about how "this project really isn't needed, and I don't need to work too hard on it." That denial turns into anger when there is a greater understanding that the change is real and necessary.

Elizabeth Kübler-Ross focused on bargaining as the next phase, and that's probably appropriate given the context of her work on death and dying. I find *depression* to be the next phase when dealing with organizational change. There's a long period where motivation to do anything new or old is significantly lowered. Depression is a focus on the worst-case scenario and that there is nothing that can be done to change it.

Bargaining, in the context of change is less of an "I'll do anything not to change" and more of a "testing the future" behavior. A typical bargaining phrase might be a "Well, maybe we could try to change this one thing, but we sure don't need to change everything." As long as bargaining comes after the phases, it's a sign that people are beginning to open up to change. Productivity really begins to rise when people have reached acceptance and understand that they are on a path toward a new future.

> **THINGS PEOPLE IN DENIAL WILL SAY**   *TRICKS OF THE TRADE*
> - Here comes the latest and greatest theme of the month.
> - This will go away.
> - Somebody really doesn't understand what has made us successful.
> - This can't work here.
> - Luckily, this won't affect me.
> - "They" need to make this work.
> - "They" don't know what they're doing.

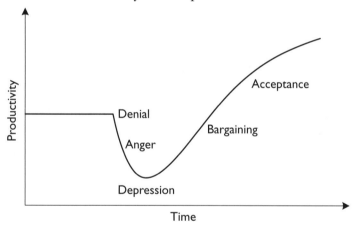

Figure 2-1. The stages of grief and change according to Kübler-Ross

While it may not be universal, nearly everybody goes through these stages in varying degrees. Even people who like the idea of change probably experience some of the feelings described here.

As they move through the initial stages of grief, you will see people:

- Focusing on what they will lose
- Sensing confusion and uncertainty
- Losing trust
- Increasing self-preservation behaviors

CAUTION

DIFFERENT PEOPLE, DIFFERENT PHASES OF CHANGE

In general, senior management will be farther along the change curve than lower levels because they have had more time to wrestle with and accept the need for change. When the CEO has moved to acceptance, the VPs might be depressed, the directors might be bargaining, and the managers might be mad, while the bottom level is in denial. Within each level, people will be in different places. It's important for you to know where people are on their change journey when you're dealing with them. If not, you will waste time on tactics people are not prepared to accept.

Again, I don't expect you to become a psychologist, but you can use this general awareness of how people experience change. When you are leading a change effort:

- Be aware that it is the rare person who will leap up and accept change. People and organizations need time to adapt to change. Many studies put the length of a typical large-scale change program at over 18 months.
- As you interact with others, be sensitive to where they are in the change process. Somebody who is angry about change is probably not ready to hear about how new ideas will help them. Somebody who has stopped being angry might well be ready to begin thinking in new ways.
- Remember your overall objective of change management: increase productivity by working to make the impact of change less disruptive to productivity (less low on the change curve) and help speed the whole process of change.

The Resistance You'll Encounter

Just as the homeostasis lesson from high school biology tells us about an organism's self-regulating systems, high school physics has lessons for change management, as well. What slows down the progress of an object in motion? Resistance. Whether it is the passive resistance of friction or the active resistance of an opposing force, resistance slows progress.

Resistance will rear its ugly head in many ways, some obvious, some subtle (see Table 2-1).

Active Resistance Behaviors	Passive Resistance Behaviors
Deliberate opposition	Withholding information or support/allowing failure to occur
Elaborate explanations regarding the risks and issues associated with the new approach	Claiming "others" won't support it
Agitating others	Delaying
Going around leaders to sabotage the project	Overcomplicating the new way

Table 2-1. Active and passive resistance during change

CONFRONTING ACTIVE RESISTANCE

TRICKS OF THE TRADE

One of the most interesting people I got advice from was a man who trained correctional officers. He shared with me that police officers are trained to use their words and force to control a situation. Correctional officers, however, must know how to use their words to control nearly every situation. The use of force is seen as a failure of one's words.

His advice on how to handle active opposition? "Isolate the leader and confront the individual directly. Deep down, even the toughest guy is usually a coward. Without fail, the leader will back down to your authority." His second piece of advice? "Be prepared."

The parallels to the business world are there. If there is a member of your organization who is actively opposing your initiative, you must isolate him or her and professionally confront them with well-prepared facts. Call this individual out to expose his or her opposition to you.

As your change initiative is no doubt blessed by a member of senior management, such individuals will back down to the authority you have been indirectly given. You and your project represent the wishes of senior management, and the opposition is well aware that they aren't resisting you, they are resisting a senior manager.

Handling Resistance

Beyond the biology and psychology, there is the simple fact that people put their own self-interest first. Each person has more loyalty to the proverbial "me" than to "them" (the company). As the saying goes, there is no I in TEAM, but there is an M and an E. Second, people wonder what would happen if the change were to fail, and leave both themselves and the company worse off. Resistance occurs out of self-preservation and fear.

Similar to the "stages of grief" model is something I call the "phases of friction." As people move through the change curve, the nature of the friction or resistance that you might experience will evolve (Table 2-2).

Stage of Change Acceptance	Phases of Friction
Denial	■ Passive resistance, if any
Anger	■ Most resistance tends to be active ■ Shock and anger are prevalent ■ Group behaviors
Depression/ Bargaining	■ Passive and active resistance ■ Inconsistent progress both forward and backward ■ Withdrawn people acting primarily as individuals ■ The "herding cats" period
Acceptance	■ Searching for solutions ■ Willingness to act as a group and support each other to move forward

Table 2-2. Phases of friction

To overcome the different types of resistance, you have to learn how *to listen to understand.* Instead of listening just long enough so you can argue with someone and prove you're right, you have to listen intently and really hear what the other person is saying and ask questions to make sure you understand his or her source of fear or concern. The more your behaviors align to the feelings people are having, the better you will be able to manage their resistance.

Table 2-3 describes other tips and techniques for dealing with people in the various stages of resistance.

Granted, this chart might be a little complex. It can be hard to remember what to do in every situation. There is, however, a very simple rule about reducing resistance to change. Every conversation about the future of your organization needs to dwell on the positive. Every conversation about the current situation or past in your organization needs to dwell on the negative.

Denial	Anger	Depression/Bargaining	Acceptance
■ Confirm understanding—require people to repeat back what they heard. ■ Be specific with assignments. ■ Establish shorter timelines. ■ Follow up frequently. ■ Be alert—a reaction is coming.	■ Be patient. ■ Get everything out in the open. ■ Accept emotional display. ■ Be realistic with promises. ■ Be nondefensive. ■ Check closely for errors. ■ Watch for subversive acts.	■ Be patient—but don't tolerate inaction. ■ Tolerate mistakes. ■ Encourage small steps forward. ■ Create opportunities for success. ■ Accept emotional displays. ■ Be supportive. ■ Gently motivate. ■ Continue direct control. ■ Involve people in all decisions. ■ Raise the bar. ■ Increase communication. ■ Be visible. ■ Spend huge amounts of time in one-on-one conversations. ■ Expect inefficiency.	■ Expect some setbacks. ■ Allow for differences in recovery time frames. ■ Reinforce hopefulness and positive steps. ■ Avoid relapses. ■ Encourage trial and error. ■ Focus on feedback, not success or failure.

Table 2-3. Dealing with resistance

DO YOUR BEST

TRICKS OF THE TRADE

I was once given a lesson about parenting. Children are like puppies; they perform best when energy is sent in their direction. Teenagers are like cats, however; they come to you when you are quiet. The corollary exists in a high change environment. Fellow employees behave at their best when you are at your best. The people in your organization are looking to you for cues on how to act. Here is a checklist for some things to keep in mind:

Resistance Management Checklist
- Be a leader, not a supervisor.
- Maintain a positive attitude.
- Consistently support your leaders with words and actions.
- Motivate by doing.
- Re-recruit your good people.
- Create a supportive work environment.
- Provide additional job know-how.
- Shoulder the burden of those who are not performing.

When you talk about the future, you can discuss what success would look like. Have the person actively engage in how good the change can be. When you talk about prior change efforts, have people focus what went wrong in those efforts. This will help you subtly get people to concentrate on a better tomorrow and commit themselves to not repeating yesterday's mistakes.

This simple rule for reducing resistance is especially important when dealing with senior management. Everything that they say about the future and past becomes "on the record." You can use their words to talk about a better future. It can be very effective when you quote it back to them. "Remember back when we started when you said...."

Why and How Major Change Initiatives Fail

Do a quick Google search on why change initiatives fail, and it seems that everybody has his or her own Top 10 (or 5 or 3) reasons. Figure 2-2 shows those cited in a survey by the Society for Human Resources Management (SHRM) in 2007, and I bet they will sound familiar. When SHRM asked people involved in a recent change initiative what their challenges were in their program, their answers pointed to three categories (see the three gray boxes below the bar chart):

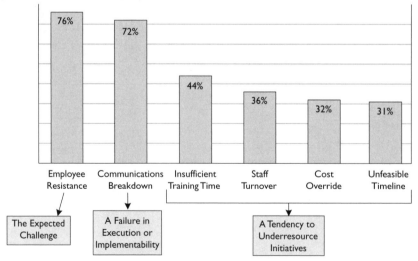

Figure 2-2. Why change initiatives fail

1. Underestimating the expected challenge
2. A failure in execution or implementability
3. Underresourcing the change effort

Basically, the people in the change initiative are saying that their organization didn't communicate enough and/or didn't allocate enough time, people, or money.

Another study showed a very different perspective on why change initiatives face challenges. In 2008 PriceWaterhouseCoopers asked CEOs about their thoughts on why change was difficult. CEOs didn't respond with answers about resource constraints or employee resistance. CEOs generally pointed to shortcomings in their staff as being the critical barrier to effective change (Figure 2-3).

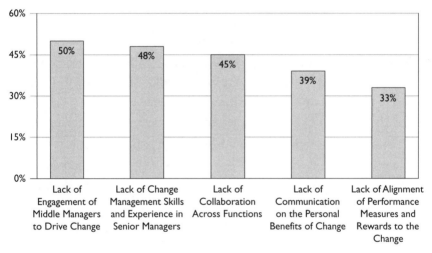

Figure 2-3. CEO perceptions of change failure

The interesting point about the managers' perspective and the CEOs' perspective is the contrast between them. Think about whom each party is holding responsible for the challenges:

CEO: Mr. Manager, you didn't have the skills to do this well.

Manager: Ms. CEO, you gave me an impossible task and then didn't give me the resources to accomplish the task.

In any case, you're the middle manager who needs to make this effort come to life. Senior management wants to be successful. You need to develop a change management plan, be very clear as to who is account-able for what parts of the plan, and ensure that the plan is executed well. The next chapters help you do just that.

Manager's Checklist for Chapter 2

☑ All change, no matter what the scale, starts at the individual level.

☑ As human beings, we have an innate tendency to prefer constancy. Understand that change runs against human nature for many people.

☑ The way people experience change is very similar to the stages of grief (denial, anger, bargaining, depression, acceptance). You don't have to be a psychologist, but being aware of how people experience change can make you a more effective change manager.

☑ There will always be resistance, and you need to be alert for both active and passive resistance behaviors.

☑ Similar to the stages of grief are the phases of friction, meaning the ways in which people show resistance alters as they go through the phases of dealing with change. The key to overcoming these phases is learning to listen to understand. Then engage the person in dis-cussing how his or her future will be better.

☑ Executives and managers basically view the failure of change effort as each other's fault, the former often citing a "lack of execution" and the latter citing "a lack of resources and support." In both cases, you need to develop a change management plan that spells out clear accountabilities.

The Vision: Starting with the End in Mind

"Would you tell me, please, which way I ought to go from here?"
"That depends a good deal on where you want to get to," said the Cat.
"I don't much care where—" said Alice.
"Then it doesn't matter which way you go," said the Cat.
"—so long as I get SOMEWHERE," Alice added as an explanation.
"Oh, you're sure to do that," said the Cat, "if you only walk long
enough."

—Lewis Carroll, *Alice in Wonderland*

The backstory woven throughout this book is that you've been asked to participate on (or even lead) a team responsible for creating a large-scale change. Executives have asked you to create a plan to take your organization from Point A to Point D. Points B and C are going to be skipped in this effort. This isn't a continuous improvement project. This is a great leap forward.

What is the first question you should ask? No, it isn't "Why me?" The first question you should ask is, "Can you tell me about Point D?"

This moment is, without a doubt, the most important point in the project for two reasons:

The first reason is obvious. You need to understand what the future will look like. Until and unless you know your destination, any path will do, as the Cat pointed out to Alice. That's why your first goal when you're put into a position of leading a change effort must be to figure out as much as you can about the future you've been charged with creating.

The second reason is less obvious. This moment also helps define some of your role on the project beyond just "change management leader." As described in Figure 3-1, your executive's answer to "where are we headed" will define how you need to work with your executive team.

If Your Executives . . .	Then Your Role Is . . .
Have a single, compelling, easily understood picture of the future with a solid rationale and plan	Ambassador to the organization
Have a single view of the future that is not easily understood	Coach to help them simplify
Have a single, compelling unified view with no plan to get there	Project manager to identify the milestones and activities that will be involved in the project
Have multiple views that are not well developed	Facilitator, to help them reach a common point of view

Figure 3-1. Your role in "where we are headed"

In this chapter, I walk you through three steps to help you define the vision for your change effort in clear, simple terms and understand how to begin to communicate that vision to others.

Step 1. Defining What the Future Looks Like

The first step in shaping the future is to define what it looks like. The usual way to do this is in the form of a vision statement, which defines in words (and perhaps pictures) where your organization is headed. It describes what will be new and different tomorrow compared to today.

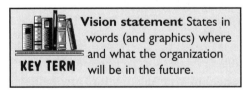

Vision statement States in words (and graphics) where and what the organization **KEY TERM** will be in the future.

It's easy to find examples of vision statements if you search the Web. For the most part, they describe the aspirations of an entire company— such as Microsoft's vision of having "a personal computer in every home running Microsoft software" or Chevron's "to be the global energy company most admired for its people, partnership, and performance." Vision statements like these are powerful because they briefly describe a clear goal or aspiration. In reading these vision statements, there is no doubt about what these companies want to achieve.

A vision statement for a change effort need not be as broad in scope as that for a whole company, but it should still clearly describe what the organization wants to achieve with the change.

CRAFTING A VISION STATEMENT

SMART

MANAGING

Don't get hung up on whether you will achieve your vision. Many organizations never achieve their vision. You will achieve far more by working toward an impossible goal than you will by working toward a modest goal.

That said, you do want to make sure management buys into your vision. If you are creating the vision on your own initiative, have the highest management level possible bless your initiative's vision. You want to be able to say, "When I was speaking to Mr. or Ms. CXO, they fully agreed with the direction we are heading." With many, a little name-dropping can certainly reduce resistance to change.

As a change leader, you may find yourself coaching senior-level executives. They may need you to honestly tell them that their vision statement isn't compelling or simple. You may also become a facilitator to help them get to a common perspective. If you need help with this step, the best place to get that help is from your human resources department. There is likely somebody in that group who has organizational development skills and can help you help your executives.

In other cases, you aren't the change agent working for the executive team. You may be the manager leading your own change program. I worked with the leader of an accounts receivable department in an industry that required a particularly labor-intensive effort in this area. Customers frequently made deductions from the vendor's invoice and a new round of negotiations began over prices. My client built what he believed to be the "perfect vision." He stated that by the year 2020 (11 years away) his department would have no deductions, no accounts receivables, and no employees.

The term *2020* was not only a year, but a way of describing the "perfect vision." With great apologies to the optometrists reading this book, the perfect vision meant his department, which was purely an administrative cost to the business, would cease to exist.

His team was more than a little surprised by his 2020 vision, but they all understood the rationale. When he moved to explain how he intended to achieve the audacious goals, he explained that 2010 was the next year and that he was looking for a series of 10 percent improvements in several key areas. People clearly understood the general direction this director was heading and what was expected in the coming year. Once he also explained that the workforce reductions could be handled through attrition, he had his team's support.

The best vision statements are:

- Compelling
- Easy to understand
- Brief
- Inspirational (energizing people to take action)
- Aspirational (describing an ideal outcome)

WHAT YOUR VISION STATEMENT ISN'T

CAUTION

Don't confuse a vision statement with two other concepts. A vision statement and a mission statement are not the same thing. Although both define actions, they serve different purposes. A mission statement describes what an organization does and is typically written in the present tense. As an example, Walmart's mission statement is "We save people money so they can live better."

A vision statement, on the other hand, describes the *destination*. It is typically written in the future tense and likely has a quantifiable outcome. Hertz lays out its ambitious goals in its vision statement as follows: "We will be the first choice brand for vehicle and equipment rental/leasing and total mobility solutions."

The second mistake to avoid with a vision statement is to make sure that it is not just a slogan. A slogan such as "Standardize, Simplify, Optimize" may help people understand and guide their actions, but it doesn't describe a future state.

Step 2. Understanding the Rationale for Change

If defining the vision is the most important moment in a project, capturing the rationale runs a close second. Given that people naturally resist change (as discussed in Chapter 2), you must be able to clearly explain the necessity for the change.

You need to understand the rationale for change—what many will call the burning platform. The story of the burning platform is simple. If you are on an offshore oil well that is on fire, there is a compelling case for action. You must act quickly.

Think of the rationale for change as the argument for doing something different. There is a logic inherent to the statement "If we do X, then Y will happen for the following reasons. Y is not satisfactory. We must achieve Z, so we are going to follow a different plan." If we stay on the burning platform, we place ourselves at great risk. To eliminate that risk, we escape in lifeboats.

SMART Goals

Once you've defined the vision and rationale for the change, you need to make your goals actionable. One way to do that is to use a tool known as SMART goals, where you define the S-M-A-R-T components of every goal or objective you set: **TOOLS**

S Strategic and Specific. The goal is linked to the vision (making it strategic) and is defined in terms specific enough that you know reaching this goal will get you closer to the vision.

M Measurable. You will able to use data to tell whether you achieved the goal.

A Attainable. The goal is achievable within the time frame you've outlined, the resources needed are within your control, and the amount of change represents enough of a stretch to be inspirational but not so much as to be impossible.

R Results-oriented. The goal describes a desired *outcome*.

T Time-bound. A goal can be SMART only if it includes a target date. Agreeing on a time frame is necessary to make sure that the effort addresses the business reasons that justify the change. Having a time frame is also necessary for making decisions about resource allocations (and vice versa).

Can you describe your organization's rationale for change in terms of a burning platform? The better you can describe the need to act, the more likely your fellow employees will follow you.

Step 3. Understanding the Approach for Achieving the Change

Another part of understanding what your company's executives want you to achieve is defining the general approach they have in mind for achieving their vision. This isn't about the detailed change management plan, because that is something you'll create. Understanding the approach means identifying the major activities that need to go on to make the change happen. How will the goals help you achieve the change? Remember the director with the 2020 vision? One of his steps was to reduce head count through attrition. He had a plan to achieve his goals.

SMART MANAGING

DEFINING THE WHEN

In my experience, the number one question people have when first learning about change is When? Before you communicate your change initiative, have a plan for the following types of "when" discussions:

- Date to assemble the project team
- Date for understanding the organizational impact of the change
- Date for announcing the change to the organization
- Target date for launch/go-live

Remember, a vision is aspirational. It reaches beyond what people are thinking about today. To attain instant credibility, a business leader and change leader should be able to speak confidently about the path he or she will follow to reach the vision. Even if the path is only loosely defined, you should talk about the process by which the path will become clear. The more information you can provide, the more confidence people will have in your ability.

Communicating the Vision

As you work with management to describe the future, you should also think about how you will communicate the vision to the rest of the organization.

The most important guiding principle here is what I call the Mother-in-Law Test: Can you take the picture of the future, the rationale for change, and the plan to achieve the change and explain it to your mother-in-law? Would she be able to quickly understand what needs to be done and why? If you can do that, you're on your way. If it doesn't make sense to her, it won't make sense to members of the organization. You have more work to do.

As you start to think about how to communicate your vision, consider your audiences. As your vision needs to be communicated to different people with different responsibilities, it helps to think about how people process information.

- For story people, use PowerPoints and verbal persuasion.
- For logic people, use persuasive written documents with numbers.

Go back and check Chapter 1. I used pictures of a change curve and a spreadsheet to build the case for change management. No doubt, conceptual people were most interested in the picture. More concrete-thinking people were drawn to the financial analysis.

PICTURING THE FUTURE

For organizations heavily loaded with conceptual/creative people, words and numbers may not be adequate for **TOOLS** communicating your vision. In that case, look for ways to literally create a picture of the future. There is a small but highly skilled group of artists/ facilitators who create anything from the simplest drawings to the most complex renderings of a situation. A Google search will easily send you in the right direction.

The Two Starting Documents

To help you communicate the vision and help your team begin acting on that vision, you need to prepare two documents before enlisting your project team. (You want to be able to recruit your team with these documents!)

Document 1. A Presentation That Tells the Story. Stories are one of the best ways to provide information. Structuring the story is the key. I have found that the SIERA method of structuring a story works well.

- **S**ummarize the situation.
- Give the **I**dea.

- **E**xplain how it works.
- **R**einforce key benefits.
- **A**sk for an easy next step.

My wife has learned how to use it effectively, as demonstrated by a recent conversation we had. She said, "You've been traveling a lot [summarize the situation]. I have an idea. You will take the kids all weekend and give me a break [the idea]. Let me explain how it works. 'You have the kids' means 'I don't have the kids' [explanation]. The benefit to you is simple. Your wife continues to remain sane [the benefits]. I assume you have no objections to this plan [asking for approval]."

FOR EXAMPLE

TAILOR THE APPROACH TO THE AUDIENCE

I spent a lot of time working with a firm that was dominated by financially oriented people. This organization needed to make a big change but was invariably frustrated by the need to rationally and financially justify the case for change. Nobody would put any numbers down because they were all afraid to have the numbers quoted—or analyzed differently by somebody else. They finally agreed to draft a document called The Strategic Rationale for Change. The case for change was so clear that the discussion of numbers boiled down to this: *It will take $200 million and take many of our best people five years to complete this effort. The benefits will come in numerous untrackable areas across our business. In the end, we don't have any other choice.*

Document 2. A Project Charter. This document contains a lot more detail than the storytelling document. It documents all the information about the direction, scope, and boundaries of the project that the team needs to keep in mind. That includes:

- Objectives
- How success will be measured
- The scope of effort required
- What is in and what is out of scope
- Critical success factors
- Initial assumptions on resources required
- Who the initial leader might be
- How the initiative might be governed

I love developing project charters. Let me describe how I handle this assignment:

- First, I sit with the executive in charge and write down all of his or her thoughts.
- Second, I capture this executive's thoughts in a document. If I don't have an answer in a particular area, I might even make up an answer.
- Third, I ask the executive for broad approval of the document.
- Fourth, I send the document to the executive's peers and other key senior-level stakeholders and then interview each executive in a one-on-one setting about the document. In doing this, I also ask one important question: Will you support me throughout the course of the project if I need your help? (The answer is always yes—and most of the time I don't even need to ask. They want to see me and the project succeed.) Those conversations, which must be kept confidential, give me all sorts of input on how to improve the document. They also tell me who is an enthusiastic supporter and who is a potential detractor and, importantly, allow me to develop a personal relationship with each of these executives.
- Fifth, I take all this feedback and change the document where there is general agreement on areas to be changed. And where there is disagreement, I bring that disagreement to the sponsoring executive for follow-up. A fractured leadership team cannot run a change program.

> ### ALIGNMENT, NOT CONSENSUS
> **TRICKS OF THE TRADE**
>
> In my interviews with executives, I focus on issues that they all comment on, not the odd issues that only one or two people mention. I tend not to follow up on the latter because my job here is *not* to shape consensus. My job is to gain alignment in where the project is going.

The Importance of a Clear Vision

I've worked with dozens of organizations as they are going through change efforts, and I can't overstate the importance of having a clear vision that is simply articulated. Doing the job well:

PROJECT CHARTER OUTLINE

TOOLS

Project charters come in many shapes and flavors, but to get you started, I've provided an outline for one below.

1. Executive Summary
   a. Project purpose, scope, and implementation overview
   b. Project sponsorship and oversight
   c. Critical success factors
   d. Expected areas of impact outside the project
   e. Timeline and financials
2. Current Situation
   a. Current organizational overview
   b. Current process overview
   c. Current technical overview
   d. Current business performance metrics
   e. Perceived opportunities with current situation
3. Project Overview and Objectives
   a. Project overview
   b. Business objectives supported by project
   c. Expected benefits
   d. Expected impacts
4. Project Scope
   a. Baseline assumptions
   b. Project dependencies
   c. Organizational scope
   d. Process scope
   e. Technical scope
   f. Scope exclusions
   g. Project deliverables
5. Implementation Strategy
   a. Project constraints
   b. Transition/cutover/go-live plan
   c. Change management and end user training approach
   d. Post go-live support plan
6. Project Organization
   a. Roles and responsibilities
   b. Resource requirements
   c. Team structure
   d. Project governance
7. Project Management Plan
   a. Project status reporting procedures
   b. Risk management plan
   c. Issue management plan

> 8. Project Timeline
> 9. Project Financials

- Provides a clear definition of success
- Enables you to continuously align people to the objectives of the program
- Serves as the basis of all future activities
- Serves as the foundation for your communication plan: It provides all of your key messages. Since the vision is authored by people who are far senior to you, as you work on the change initiative, you pick up the authority of these excutives.

If you *don't* do a good job of defining and explaining the vision, your project team will be operating without a common definition of success. You will be constantly relitigating what should be happening. You will waste a lot of time and effort going in directions that end up being fruitless or inappropriate.

BE CONVINCED OR GET OUT

If you have worked with your management on the vision for the future and you aren't convinced it's realistic or achievable, my best advice is that you find a new place to work. I mean that seriously. There are three simple reasons why: First, if the executives can't convince you, how will you convince others? Second, if they can't convince you, maybe they have an impossible vision. Third, if they can't motivate you, you will not perform well in helping them achieve their vision. In any of these three situations, the outcome is not good for you, and you should get out sooner rather than later.

Manager's Checklist for Chapter 3

☑ The most important point in a project is the first question you should ask: What will the future look like?

☑ The answers to this question will help you define your role in the process.

☑ A vision statement is not a mission statement. The vision statement describes the destination, not the purpose.

☑ The second most important point is laying out the rationale, or business case, for change. You have to describe a compelling reason that will convince people that going in this direction is the right thing to do for themselves personally as well as for the company.

☑ When communicating the vision, it should be able to pass the mother-in-law test. You should be able to quickly, simply, and effectively make the case for change to someone who knows nothing about the situation.

☑ To support your communication efforts, you need two documents: a presentation that tells the story and a project charter.

Creating
Sustainable
Change

Any transition serious enough to alter your definition of self will require not just small adjustments in your way of living and thinking but a full-on metamorphosis.

—Martha Beck
Sociologist and Author

The previous chapter got you thinking about the endpoint of your change initiative. This is the vision that shapes your path. As almost anybody who has made a New Year's resolution will tell you, it's easy to start work on a vision, but making it stick is hard. This chapter shares the secrets of making large-scale change sustainable. In my experience, the key is getting the scope correct. I'm going to show you that if you want to change one aspect of an organization's strategic direction, process, or structure, you need to make sure all the elements work in tandem. If you don't, you'll end up just like the out-of-shape guys who haven't used their gym memberships since the third week of January.

Let me share a business story that demonstrates my point. A client once asked me to help her company design a series of sales reports that would effectively track the organization's performance. The client was having difficulty growing the business and was convinced that more reporting and controls would help manage the salespeople and drive higher sales. I started the project by inquiring about the current situation:

- Which parts of the business are you having difficulty growing?
- What are the challenges in managing your sales organization's selling performance?
- What reports do you currently use to manage the sales organization?

The client's answers weren't very specific. I asked more directly: "Please show me the reports you use to calculate your salespeople's bonuses or commissions."

The answers suddenly became clear. "We don't have any good reports that show individual performance. Our former CEO didn't believe in paying our sales organization based on individual performance. He believed that we are all in this together, so the sales organization should be paid based on how the whole company performed."

I'm not a compensation expert, but I do have experience with sales organizations and salespeople. They're certainly team-oriented people, but every salesperson expects to be rewarded, at least partly, based on individual contribution. I changed direction. "I realize you think you have an issue with reporting and the controls you have in place in your company, but do you think you might also have a compensation issue? Even if you had the right reports, are your incentives aligned with your company goals?"

At this point, the project became more complex. The client realized that she not only needed a way to track individual sales, but a reward program as well. It was like going to the doctor and hearing the words "diet *and* exercise." There isn't a choice between dieting and exercise. You must do both. To improve sales and profits, this company needed a comprehensive solution. Designing a few reports was only the beginning.

Aligning Your Efforts

Step back for a minute and think about change programs. The objectives are typically clear. There's usually a people element and a process element to a project. But the typical project starts as work in only one of those areas. I often hear things like, "We have a new area of focus," "We need to reengineer our processes," or "We need to reorganize our business."

I'd assert that a change program won't be successful unless there is *alignment* among objectives, processes, and people.

If you align all the pieces affected by the change, you'll create something that's hard to break. Remember that classic Aesop fable about the bundle of sticks? An old man told his sons to break a bundle of sticks, but none succeeded. He then had them untie the bundle, each take one stick, and break it. They did it easily.

An organizational change effort with all the elements aligned is like creating a bundle of sticks: It is harder to damage. All the communication plans, stakeholder management programs, and end user training sessions won't help an organization whose objectives, processes, and people are out of alignment.

FOCUS ON THE BUSINESS RESULTS

TRICKS OF THE TRADE

When you enter into a change project, you need to think purposefully. You really aren't there to execute a change plan; your role is to be a change agent who brings about a specific business result. You aren't there to perform activities. You're there to obtain a result. If the organization isn't on the path to achieving that result, you need to change your activities.

When you think in terms of outcomes—and not activities—you align yourself with how people two levels up on the organization chart think. They are less concerned with the processes and structures that need to change and the tactics that help the people move through change. They care about measurable *results*.

Ensuring that your thinking is outcome oriented and comprehensive enables you to consider all the factors that drive long-term organizational performance. It also serves you well with senior leadership.

What does alignment mean in terms of creating sustainable change? Figure 4-1 illustrates my company's Organizational Alignment Model™, which we designed as a guide for organizations going through change. It shows the full scope of issues you need to address to obtain a successful change initiative. Think of it as a checklist of all the areas where there should be common direction.

The model has nine components that fall into three clusters—objectives, processes, and people—coordinated around one central element, *change leadership*. In this chapter, we review these 10 areas and conclude with a discussion of the model as a whole.

The most successful, enduring change initiative is the one that con-

Figure 4-1. Organizational Alignment Model

tains activity in all 10 areas and integrates all activities. To begin, here is an overview of the three clusters of components.

Objectives

There are two components under objectives: strategies and culture. I once worked for a major consumer products company that had one overriding objective: growth. The company started with one very successful product. Eighty percent of the time a consumer would leave the store purchasing this company's product over another brand. Knowing this couldn't last and to protect my employer's interests, we embarked on a diversification strategy. We wanted more engines of growth.

As time passed, memories faded, CEOs changed, and we were presented with a new objective. One Monday morning we came into the office to see a new mission statement. We were no longer about diversification and growth. We were now all about maximizing the profit from our flagship product.

The people who worked for the non-flagship brands were, understandably, nervous—and with good reason. The CEO began

Figure 4-2. The objectives cluster

selling off all the other brand lines. He also drove changes, such as reducing the amount of product in each box by 25 percent and the price by only 10 percent. Our company made a lot more money, and consumers remained with the brand.

This kind of change was hard for employees to understand and accept. Formerly, the company used "excess" capital to grow. Now, however, the company turned those profits into short-term benefits for the shareholders.

I tell this story to illustrate that whether a company is leading a major change effort itself or working with a consultant, the following questions are fundamental:

1. What are the objectives? What is the rationale supporting these objectives? How big a leap are these objectives from current practice? Are there interim goals? Simply put, the underlying concept is understanding the definition

DO YOUR MESSAGES ALIGN SMART **WITH YOUR OBJECTIVES?**
A client once complained to me that company costs were out of control. I looked at the MANAGING last CEO letter to employees and saw that it mentioned market share 18 times and cost control only once. Was it any wonder that employees saw more importance in growing revenue than in controlling costs? Make sure that any messages your managers and executives send are the right messages and that the incentives you put in place are aligned to your true objectives.

of success. Your vision and the related subobjectives need to be aligned and consistent.

2. What are the new strategies? What strategies will you use to reach the objectives? What is the same as or different from previous strategies? What has to happen to make the new strategy a reality?

Michael Porter wrote a fantastic book titled *Competitive Strategy* (The Free Press). In it he talks about the three basic organizational strategies. A company can choose to compete primarily on price, on quality, or on how it differs from other companies. The three main mass merchandise retailers in the United States demonstrate those three strategies well. Walmart competes on its low-price image. Target competes on quality. The typical Target is a nicer shopping experience and, in many departments, filled with products that are slightly more upscale than Walmart's. To compete against those two larger businesses, Kmart is left to compete based on things like unique geography.

Expanding the thinking to retailers such as Dollar General and Family Dollar, the point of difference becomes clearer. Their difference is having smaller stores that allow them to be in more places than Target and Walmart. It's a great strategy to use to compete against those giants.

So the question to you as the change leader for your organization is, Can I describe our strategy in simple terms such as price, product, or differentiation? I recommend you work hard to do this. If you can help people understand your company's strategies in these clear and easy-to-understand terms, you'll be fantastic at moving change forward.

3. What needs to happen in the culture? Company culture is one of the toughest areas for a change agent to address. You need to understand how the current culture works for and against your organization's proposed new direction. You have to think through such questions as:

- Does the organization value results or the people who create results?
- Is action more valued than consensus?
- Do your peers take ownership or seek approval?
- Does the organization value individualism, or does it value teamwork?
- Are people willing to take risks, or do they tend to avoid risks?
- Is management process oriented, or does it value flexibility and agility?

Once you understand the complexity of the organization's culture, you can begin to think about whether your change initiative can help move the culture in a particular direction. The answer is probably "absolutely." Can a set of tactics create cultural change? Probably not.

Truth be told, changing an organization's culture usually means having a critical mass of leaders who want to take a new approach away from how things are done in the current culture. That critical mass usually comes from new leadership, and chances are, you don't have that charter.

COUNTERACT YOUR CULTURE

Because it is so difficult to create cultural change in a short time, I tend to limit my involvement in comprehensive cultural change assignments. I recommend that you avoid signing up for a culture change project.

This isn't to say that I don't use culture to my advantage. The martial arts provide a lesson on how to do this. Several of the martial arts teach you how to use the weight and force of an opponent to your advantage. If someone is punching you, it isn't a great idea to block that punch. It is far better to grab the punching arm and pull the person toward you. The person's momentum will work to your advantage. Apply the same concept to changing an organization's culture. I try to use culture as an accelerant to change.

Let me give you an example. Think about a bureaucratic, consensus-driven organization. This type of organization is typically oriented toward the success of teams and tends not to value individual initiative. Your job would be to highlight the accomplishments of teams throughout the change effort. An opposite example is also true. A "lean and mean" organization that values entrepreneurialism typically holds the accomplishments of individuals in high regard. Your "martial arts" approach would be to constantly and publicly praise the heroic achievements of individuals in the effort.

Throughout large change efforts, people try to understand the values that the company is moving toward. What you choose to publicize can accelerate your progress.

Because it's so difficult to create comprehensive cultural change in a short time, I tend, as a consultant, to limit culture work during change projects to "martial arts" terms. I focus my work so that the force of the culture forms an accelerant to the change required.

If an organization values teamwork over individualism, the change team must focus on team accomplishments throughout the change effort. The same can be said about stories of decision making. Did somebody make a direct decision, or did somebody work hard to build consensus on a particular point?

The more people see the path toward change as having many of the same attributes as how they currently operate, the more likely they are to want to go down that path.

Processes

Sometimes a consultant can be thankful for not working on a project. Early in my career my company was asked to recommend to a large organization how we could help them implement a new organizational design for their sales group. The company believed its sales organization needed to be downsized.

We laid out a detailed organizational plan that involved an analysis of its business trends, the complexity of its product line, the work it took to sell the company's products, and the composition of its customer base. Their response to our recommendations was polite but firm: "We've already decided on all the jobs in the top three levels of the new organization."

My manager at the time provided insights that taught me some valuable lessons:

- Always define the work to be done before you define who will do the work. An architect would say, "Form follows function."
- The actual work of selling is done by the bottom layers of the organization chart. This company's leaders had decided the top of the organization chart. Cutting costs meant cutting the people who actually did the work.
- Define the work before you define the management structure.

There are three concepts that comprise the broader concept of the way people work: processes, systems, and controls.

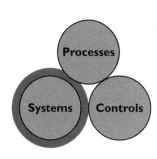

Figure 4-3. The processes cluster

Processes. A *business process* is the sequence of steps that convert a set of inputs into a set of outputs. For example, an accounts payable department receives a vendor invoice as an input. It performs a set of activities to convert that input into a payment to that vendor. That payment is the output. A business process is the actual work people do, step by step. Note that *processes* are not positioned at one of the triangle's points—as *objective* and *people* are—and yet I'm discussing it as one of the three main clusters. You will see why later in the chapter as the nine components also align to tiers of action.

There is a robust field of experts who focus on business process management and ensure that processes are lean and deliver high-quality, consistent results. The heart of many transformation efforts involves process redesign or reengineering.

As a change management leader, you should think about:

> **Business process management** Optimizing processes so they are efficient and effective. You may hear terms such as "reengineering," "lean," or "six sigma" related to process optimization.
>
> **KEY TERM**

- The specific changes in how people will work
- How people will perceive the changes in their work
- All the places that document the ways of working—and all the places that documentation needs to be updated
- Training for those who will be affected by the change
- The education of not only those who directly participate in the process, but also of those who rely on the new process
- How your organization can reap the benefits of the changed process as quickly as possible

Systems. I use the term *systems* to mean the organization's information technology (IT) systems. How does the company's technology support or hinder the company's objectives, strategies, and processes? How do you manage the areas where it doesn't fit the company's purposes?

There are two ways to think about systems: (1) Are you changing the other eight areas and creating changes to the IT systems, or (2) are you changing the IT systems and impacting the rest of the business?

When an organization changes its business model, reengineers processes, or restructures itself, projects frequently get slowed down by challenges associated with modifying IT systems. Be sure you work with your IT team to develop a timeline in which they can work.

When an organization changes its IT systems, the change differs in two significant ways from a typical project:

1. User definitions and security access are highly specialized areas where experienced IT help is required. Depending on the standards in your organization, you must provide highly specific access to the system and create job profiles based on those decisions.
2. Going live with a new IT system is only part of the challenge. How do you provide post-go-live support for new users, employee job changes, and system upgrades? Many organizations build some form of super-user network for the post-go-live world. Building and main-

KEY TERM **Post-Go-Live support** Those processes and structures put in place to enable employees to operate productively after change implementation. Typically, a major part of an IT system implementation involves a technical help desk function and a means to answer "how do I perform a task" questions. Although plenty of training is provided before a new system goes live, you must support people after that go-live.

A robust "how do I perform a task" process gives organizations an important competency. When a system is modified or an employee is hired, there is a network of skilled staff who can be deployed to help users get up to speed quickly.

taining that structure is a relatively simple effort, but it is rarely a small effort.

Controls. Controls range from the simplest, such as the reports example from the beginning of this chapter, to the complex, such as concepts used by an audit professional. Controls are the tools and mechanisms that management uses to govern activities. Policy manuals, work instructions, and compliance reports are all examples of controls.

There's an old story about getting a stubborn donkey to do something. The owner ties a carrot to the end of a stick, gets on the donkey, and dangles the carrot in front of it. The donkey walks and walks, trying to reach that elusive carrot. If the donkey isn't hungry, the owner always has the

SMART MANAGING **PAY ATTENTION TO YOUR AUDIENCE'S NEEDS**
The reality is many of us work in a global environment. This means there are billions of people who don't speak or read English. Recently, I traveled to China for a client who insisted that each employee sign a statement indicating he or she had "read and understood" the documentation for each business process he or she used. However, my client had published its business process documentation in English and only English—and built an English-only system to track the documentation and "read and understood" sign-offs. Obviously, the controls weren't going to be effective.

As a change leader, you need to take on the burden of making sure people successfully perform their work. It might mean working in another language, or it could mean something far more basic. There are organizations that face literacy challenges. It's worth your time to find out how people best receive information.

stick to provide "alternative encouragement" (control). Controls, whether we like them or not, are the sticks that ensure organizational performance.

People

Now that what has to be done is defined, it's time to address the people side of the operation.

Structure. Typically, a change professional neither defines the process by which people work nor sets the organizational structure. Change professionals deal with the implications of changing those structures and provide impartial advice on how to optimize structures. They also work to ensure that the processes and

Figure 4-4. The people cluster

structures work well together. In addition, they may recommend reducing the number of managerial levels and increasing managerial spans of control. Change professionals also address the organizational design that's created to provide an executive with experience in a particular area. In this case, they work to ensure processes are designed to reflect the management configuration.

People. When thinking about the objectives you need to reach, ask yourself, "Do we have the right people with the right skills in the right numbers in the right places?" It's likely the answer to some or all of these issues will be "no." As a change professional, your job is to ensure that your organization is aware of the issues and has a plan in place to address the gaps. People may resist or even sabotage a change if they fear they will be seen as incompetent in the new system. As a change

---

COMMUNICATE, COMMUNICATE, COMMUNICATE!   **SMART**

I once helped a company go through a major reorganization, and we did a terrific job of explaining to the affected employees what their new jobs entailed. The trouble was, we didn't tell the rest of the organization about those new job responsibilities. As a result, **MANAGING** employees with *new* job responsibilities were still being contacted about their *old* job responsibilities. We put the right structures in place, but we exhibited poor control over the system by failing to expand our communication about work responsibilities under the reorganized structure.

leader, your job is to give them confidence by assuring them that they will have the training and skills to be as successful *after* the change.

Rewards. Many change initiatives I've seen can be characterized like this: An executive says, "We have a new objective. From now on, we're all going to turn left." Meanwhile, the incentives are still written to reward people who "turn right."

Let's return to the company with the profitable flagship brand and new CEO that we discussed at the beginning of this chapter. When he arrived, the organization was growing through diversification. Naturally, the sales force had targets and bonus payments for each product line, and it was important that each line receive attention. However, the new CEO changed directions, ordering that all attention go toward the flagship brand. The sales organization ignored the directive because its pay was still linked to performance on other brands. The CEO was not going to get what he wanted until he changed the compensation plan.

SMART MANAGING

WHY PEOPLE CHOOSE TO ACT

I received some advice on my first day of work in the professional world. I had a job in sales, and the regional sales manager said, "People do things for one of three reasons: hope of gain, fear of loss, or ego. Your job is to figure out what drives each person." Sure, the first two reasons drive many behaviors, but public praise is often a more powerful incentive. As a change leader, you want to "catch people in the act" of doing the new "right" thing and hold them up as examples of leadership, innovation, and excitement. Use your communication plan to publicize those who help the organization move in the right direction. This appeals to the egos within your workplace and will work wonders.

This lack of alignment between objectives and rewards is not new and is often overlooked in change management efforts. Look at your incentives and make sure they encourage people to perform in ways consistent with your new objectives. If they don't align, the incentives need to be modified or your change won't be sustained.

Don't forget, however, most incentives are not monetary. Many organizations recognize performance less formally. "On the spot" awards for an outstanding task, positive feedback in a review, or a verbal or written thank-you can go a long way in encouraging exceptional performance.

The Glue: Change Leadership

The glue that holds all these pieces together is change leadership. I deliberately use the word *leadership* instead of *management*.

I take the perspective that you don't manage change; you *lead* change. That means getting out in front, providing direction and guidance, being actively involved, and setting an example for others. If you just sit in an office and tell others what to do, your change efforts will be less effective.

Change Leadership

Figure 4-5. The leadership component

WHAT DOES AN ORGANIZATIONAL CHANGE MANAGEMENT PROFESSIONAL DO?

TRICKS OF THE TRADE

- Understands the change being implemented and the groups being impacted
- Creates a change strategy appropriate to the situation
- Ensures that the change initiative sponsors demonstrate active and visible leadership over the program and that they receive the support and coaching necessary for success
- Develops communication plans and deliverables to create awareness and understanding among initiative stakeholders
- Anticipates points of resistance and develops plans to address those concerns
- Provides an effective feedback loop to continuously gain input from those involved in the effort
- Ensures work team structures are designed and implemented with adequate role definitions, responsibilities, operating guidelines, and relationships with other work teams
- Ensures there exists a robust governance process to guide the effort and engage leadership in the success of the effort
- Manages the stakeholder community by continuously communicating the results of ongoing readiness assessments, issues, and recommendations
- Identifies risks to the organization's operation and implements risk management plans
- Supports employee-facing managers with appropriate tools and information so they can lead their teams through the change process.
- Ensures delivery of user education and training
- Provides appropriate support to affected personnel at go-live and post-transition

- Facilitates documentation of work performed and lessons learned for use with subsequent change efforts

What Skills Are Required?
- Ability to influence individuals without having a position of direct authority
- Verbal, written, and presentation communication skills
- Facilitation and coaching skills
- Courage to deal with senior leadership
- Strategic agility and comfort with ambiguity
- Flexibility
- Ability to prioritize, plan, and manage a project
- Cross-cultural sensitivity

What Experiences Are Needed to Be Successful?
- Corporate communications
- Organizational development
- Systems implementation
- Training design, development, delivery, and administration
- Business process improvement methods such as Lean and Six Sigma
- Cross-functional coordination

Making Change Sustainable

As you've seen, there are a lot of components to a change effort. The fact is that the more tightly you integrate these pieces, the more coherent and coordinated the effort is, the easier the transition from old to new. I know the to-do list may look daunting, but if you take the time up front to think through and work on all these areas, you have a better chance of creating something lasting for your organization.

Now that we understand the nine components in our model for sustainable change, it's time to fine tune and explore how they interact with one another in a more dynamic context. Step back and look at the entire model as a whole (see Figure 4-6), and note the following key orientation points:

1. **Change Leadership** is the magnetic force that holds all nine components together. Back to the example at the beginning of the chapter, change leadership is what facilitated the controls and rewards to work together. Reports without rewards would have been ineffective, and so would the new compensation system without controls to manage it. Similarly, change leadership pulls together other compo-

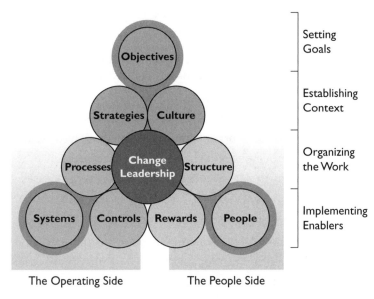

The Operating Side   The People Side

Figure 4-6. The complete model: putting it all together

nents that might otherwise seem to operate in silos and makes them interact with one another toward the overall desired outcome. Change leadership touches and interacts with each of the nine components.

2. The various latitudinal tiers of the triangle (shown in Figure 4-6) represent the four tiers of action—and show how the components contribute to each action. Note that the top two tiers—**Setting Goals** and **Establishing Context**—are components most typically completed by senior management. Senior management is usually the only group with access to these two components. The bottom two tiers—**Organizing the Work** and **Implementing Enablers**—are typically those that the director or middle manager levels influence and activate.

3. The components falling on the left side of the triangle pertain to the **Operating Side** of the company, whereas those on the right side of the triangle comprise the **People Side** of the company. Note that change leadership and objectives fall on both sides. They are the elements necessary for both.

4. The elements are arranged as a triangle to show that the lower components support the upper components, and the upper components

shape what happens with the lower components. Going from the top down, it's clear that:

- At the top tier—**Setting Goals**—everything that happens in an organization should be driven by the objectives.
- The second tier—**Establishing Context**—involves using culture to shape behaviors and using strategies to drive actions.
- The third tier—**Organizing the Work**—involves creating the necessary processes and structure to assign projects to work teams.
- At the fourth tier—**Implementing Enablers**—processes are enabled by systems and controls. The organization design, in turn, relies on the people assigned to it and how you reward them.

Using this model helps ensure that your business processes and people are connected to your leader's vision for the organization, and that nothing essential has been overlooked.

Manager's Checklist for Chapter 4

☑ Align all the pieces of the change effort to create something that's hard to break.

☑ The Organizational Alignment Model™ outlines the 10 components that need to be in alignment, grouped in three clusters—(1) objectives, (2) processes, (3) people—plus a central element, (4) change leadership. The model also has embedded in it an operating side and a people side, the levels of action (executive, middle management, frontline), and building the basic foundation (the bottom circles), which supports the other elements.

☑ Make sure your messages align with your objectives.

☑ Decide *what* needs to be done before you decide *who* will do it.

☑ Communicate all aspects of the change plan so people know where they and their coworkers fit in the future configuration.

☑ Change your employees' incentives if you want to change your outcomes.

☑ The glue that holds the pieces together is change *leadership*, not only change management. You need to be out in front, providing direction and guidance and actively setting an example.

The ASPIRE Framework for Change

Have a plan. Follow the plan, and you'll be surprised how successful you can be. Most people don't have a plan. That's why it's easy to beat most folks.

—Paul "Bear" Bryant
Former Football Coach, University of Alabama

A few years ago, I worked with a U.S.-based subsidiary of a German company. The company was beginning an initiative to redesign its supply chain and replace many of the core systems that supported the company. I was there to deliver change management training for the managers. At the end of the week of training, I was asked if I had any recommendations to make to the CFO. I suggested the organization needed a comprehensive, structured change management plan. A little change management training was not going to be enough. He had two responses:

1. "We do not need change management. We are a German company. They will do what I say."
2. After deciding to not discuss national stereotypes, I reminded him that his employees were not German. His response: "Okay. You have one week to prove to me that we need change management."

I immediately moved into action and surveyed the company's top 25 people about the initiative. The good news was that 95 percent of top

NEVER ASSUME

CAUTION Although the story of the misalignment of the German company's management seems unbelievable, there isn't an experienced consultant who doesn't have similar examples from his or her clients. Such stories may sound far-fetched, but they aren't. The lesson for you is to never assume people will automatically understand the reasons for your change management plan.

management indicated that the initiative was under way. Unfortunately, they were actually unclear about why they were undertaking this initiative. It just seemed like a good idea. In other words, the executives of a $1 billion company didn't know why they were working on a huge initiative.

I presented my findings one week later. The CFO was disappointed in his team and in himself for not knowing they were unclear. He realized that he had almost led the group into a major dysfunctionality. He would have communicated the wrong message. Then management would have communicated the wrong message to frontline workers. The project team would have designed the wrong solution. People would have been confused, and morale and business results would have suffered.

This story illustrates several points, but the most relevant for this chapter is the concept of "logical ordering." The German CFO would have implemented his initiatives before he understood the current attitudes of his workforce. There is an order by which you execute a change initiative. Step 2 must follow Step 1. Step 3 must follow Step 2. If you execute the steps out of order, you invite inefficiencies, mistakes, and problems. At worst, the project will fail and the business will suffer.

The framework my company uses is called ASPIRE.

ASPIRE is a structured flow of a change management process with one goal: to keep the project leader and initiative organized. It isn't magic, but it is logical, and it's:

- **Universal.** The same steps apply whether you reorganize a department or relocate a facility. The nature of the change doesn't alter the flow of activities.
- **Cyclical.** You may go through several minicycles of execution. For example, you may execute a communication plan with executives and

find yourself at the Evaluate Effectiveness phase, yet you are only beginning the Assessing the As-Is phase with frontline employees.

- **Scalable.** ASPIRE can be used on the largest as well as the smallest of initiatives.

ASPIRE BY ANY OTHER NAME ...

A structured methodology such as ASPIRE may be familiar to an IT professional. The typical IT project has phases along the following lines:

- Current state assessment
- Future state design
- Development
- Testing
- Training
- Conversion to the new system
- Support

There's no question that IT professionals follow a process when upgrading a computer system. If they developed an IT system while they were designing it, surely they would need to redo some of the development work as requirements changed. Training on a system that hasn't been tested leads to frustrated users. For a systems professional, changing the order of the steps is courting failure.

For most of this chapter, I walk through the six steps of ASPIRE, with special emphasis on assessment, because it greatly impacts your ability to do a good job on the remaining ASPIRE steps. But first, I want to set the stage by talking about your role in approaching this framework.

You're the Architect

The best analogy I've found for describing the role of a change leader is to compare it to an architect's building process. An architect first unearths the client's vision, then studies the existing structure (if there is one) and its surroundings, and finally clarifies the timing and budget. An architect works with the client to set standards for success and design what the final building will look like.

During the two initial steps, Assess the As-Is and Set Goals, equivalent to the AS of ASPIRE, the architect has little skin in the game. He or she is carrying on a dialogue with the client and eliciting necessary information.

If the client gives the architect an impossible goal, that's the client's problem. The architect may be able to help shape the vision, but only if the client is willing to listen.

Now skip ahead to the Implement step. The architect hands over blueprints to the contractor, who does the implementing—hiring subcontractors, purchasing supplies, building the structure. The architect is in the background, advising and supporting, perhaps changing the blueprints if necessary.

The same is true for the final two steps, RE (Recognize Results and Evaluate Effectiveness). The architect needs to be involved to know whether the outcomes match the plan, but it is not the architect who does the recognizing and evaluating. That's the client's responsibility.

There's only one step that an architect's contribution will be measured against: Plan. The architect (and especially a change architect) may be responsible for seeing that all the ASPIRE steps happen, but he or she is only held accountable for the plan.

There's no one there to help you out, either. When you create a change management plan, hopefully you will have good information to draw from, but it's you and a blank sheet of paper. I go into the details of what goes into the plan in Chapters 6 through 10, but let's first get you familiar with the full ASPIRE framework.

SMART

MANAGING

FACILITATING CHANGE

Change management practitioners *facilitate* change; they don't *create* change. They are like architects. They *conceive* plans; they don't *build* structures.

Staff functions play an important role in creating and supporting business readiness, but they should not be held accountable for change. Creating readiness for change relies on the manager's ability to lead his or her people. The change practitioner's job is to equip line managers with ways to understand the change activities of the change initiative. A structure like ASPIRE guides line managers through the process.

ASPIRE Overview

There are six steps in the ASPIRE model (Figure 5-1). Let's look at each one.

Step 1: Assess the As-Is

Previous chapters talked about how change management is the way the

Figure 5-1. ASPIRE framework

organization moves from Point A (where it is today) to Point D (where you want to be in the future). Chapter 3 helped you define the vision for Point D. The first step in preparing for the change is to find out more about Point A so you can make good choices about how to support your organization through the transition.

The primary As-Is Assessment relates to current business performance metrics. At its core, your change initiative focused on changing business performance. All other change attributes are secondary. It is vital that you document, and gain agreement to, the current state. The details are unique to your specific project, but some typical examples are shown in Table 5-1.

Many change practitioners are wary of documenting business performance metrics. I often hear, "I can't affect metric X, and I'll get fired if we don't achieve the goal." In some cases, this is true. If it is true, I suggest finding a new place to work. If you can be fired for something you can't control, you work for the wrong management.

Most times, however, the change manager has misunderstood his or her role. The change manager is the person who enables line managers to create change. It is line management that's responsible for communicating,

Project Type	Key Performance Indicator
Organizational Realignment	■ Functional costs as a percent of revenue ■ Managerial spans of control ■ Number of layers of management
Process Redesign	■ Cycle time to complete ■ Reduction in errors/defects ■ Reduction in process costs
System implementation	■ System cost as a percent of revenue ■ Payback period on system investment

Table 5-1. Example indicators of the current state

creating understanding, engaging stakeholders, and making the business decisions that impact business results. Think of yourself as the personal trainer to somebody trying to lose weight. Ultimately, your client has to do the work. You are only there to guide them through the process.

Understand that Point A requires a baseline assessment of the key players'—leaders, managers, employees—perception of the change before you begin to implement it. Simply put, participants' perceptions are your reality when

DOCUMENTING THE CURRENT STATE

CAUTION

The current state performance metrics is one of the easiest concepts to overlook when working on your project. You might think, "Everybody knows our current state," and you would be correct. But, my experience tells me that when you get to the end point, there will be great disagreement over what the starting point was. Document your current state—and date it.

you're the change sponsor. You need to know:

■ Whether your leadership is aligned around the vision, goals, and approach
■ What works in favor of the change, and what works against it
■ Who are the potential leaders or blockers among the people and groups involved in making or who will be affected by the change

Having this information will help you select the right strategies and tactics to build awareness and understanding during the early stages. In a similar fashion, this baseline will prove invaluable as you work to engage employees in later stages. Your baseline analysis of people's perceptions can become a metric by which you measure shifting attitudes—and the degree of buy-in—at various points during the change process.

An assessment of the participants' perspectives also helps you diagnose work-related issues and overall organizational climate, anticipate potential reactions such as resistance or hostility, define team- or manager-specific problems that may prevent or hinder success, and make good decisions involving communication, training, and other change-enabling programs. The assessment puts you in a good place to bolster employee morale and reduce declines in productivity during the initiative.

As part of the assessment, you need to determine what project structures and change enablers you have at your disposal, such as:

■ Resources (staffing, timing, financial)
■ Governance
■ As-is documentation (including job descriptions, organization charts, and process documentation)
■ Project management processes

More details on how to do a broad-scale assessment at the beginning of a major change project are given in a later section of this chapter.

Step 2: Set Standards

The overall goal of your change effort is defined by your vision of Point D and the business case you've compiled for the change (see Chapter 3). The question you face as you begin to plan for implementation is: How will you know if you've arrived?

Once you've gathered your information in the Assess phase, you're in a stronger position to specify the goals for your end state. What specifically will be different from Point A to Point D? Think about setting goals based on two categories:

1. **Outcome goals:** These are the goals that capture the underlying purpose of the change effort. These goals become the road map for your change project. They should include outcome-oriented goals (financial results, gains in productivity, cost savings) as well as operating principles (transparency, process efficiencies, or other items important to the company and sponsors).

2. **Enabling goals:** Enabling goals are achievements necessary to secure the final outcome goals. A large-scale system implementation might have a goal such as a reduction in inventory or in systems maintenance costs. A large-scale IT system implementation might have a goal such as the launch of a structured approach to employee training.

As you document your goals, remember the lesson from Chapter 3: Define your goals in SMART terms. Make them specific, measurable, attainable, results-oriented, and time-bound. The more fully and specifically your goals are defined, the more apt you are to achieve them.

Step 3: Plan Programs

In ASPIRE's third step, you use your vision and the knowledge you gained about the current state (including people's attitudes) to craft your change management plan. The shape and contents of your plan depend on the type of change you want to create, the size of your organization, the cultures you're working with, the readiness of different parts of the organization, and so on.

This work can be daunting, even scary at times. Think back to the analogy of a change manager as architect: Planning is where the architect faces a blank piece of paper. Often there's nothing more intimidating than starting from scratch. But it's probably why you were asked to get involved. Senior managers feel you're the most capable person to take on the challenge, to get a plan written on that proverbial blank sheet of paper.

I will address, in more detail, the planning of your change effort and the strategies required in Chapters 6 through 10. For the time being, know that your plan comprises five major strategies:

1. Generate awareness
2. Create understanding
3. Ensure engagement
4. Use leverage
5. Measure results

Step 4: Implement Initiatives

Sticking with our architect metaphor, in the Implement Initiatives step you hand off your blueprint to the contractor. With only a few exceptions, your

---

ENGAGE OTHERS IN THE PLANNING   **SMART**

Far too often, a change team does all the planning, then springs the
final product on the people who are expected to make the change.
If you expect your employees to embrace the coming change,
they need to understand the program completely and, ideally,   **MANAGING**
believe they have ownership. That's why you must make every effort to
engage affected individuals in *planning the program*. They will be apt to have a
stronger connection to the change and to maintain steady focus on the tasks
at hand because they understand the top- or bottom-line implications.

---

role at this point is to support the work of others, not do it yourself. But you
could be called on to be anything from a speechwriter or emcee to a coor-
dinator and clarifier. Your work isn't done—far from it. You're just taking a
backseat to the people doing the implementation.

WHY YOU NEED TO TAKE A BACK SEAT   **TRICKS OF THE TRADE**

Surveys have shown that employees don't want to hear about a
change effort from the HR group or a change management team.
They want to be told about—and guided through—a change by the
people they know best and have the most trust in—their immediate manager or supervisor. So even if you want to stay front and center, or if others
ask you to, it's a bad idea. Part of your implementation plan should include
preparing frontline and middle level managers to lead the change.

Step 5: Recognize Results

As the change implementation unfolds, you must ensure that there are
clear rewards—or consequences—for employees whose behavior either
supports or thwarts success. This is the step of your project where you
tell people what you want more of and what you want less of.

The successful execution of a change effort ultimately requires people
to change their work behaviors. It stands to reason that performers—if
evaluated on how they embrace change—should be recognized and
rewarded if their behaviors warrant. On the other hand, those who don't
embrace the change—or are slow or reluctant to do so—should understand the consequences of their actions.

When reinforcing results, change owners will quickly learn that the
evaluation and recognition of performers requires skill, tact, sensitivity,

and, most of all, leadership. An honest and forthright appraisal of an employee's performance relative to an organizational change should lead to acknowledging positive behaviors, strengthening motivation and ownership within teams and across functions, and eliminating pockets of apathy, reticence, resistance, or active opposition.

Step 6: Evaluate Effectiveness

During your change program you need to track the following elements: the status of your outcome goals, the status of your enabling goals, the activities you planned, and the activities you performed. There are four possible outcomes:

1. **Implemented as planned, got the desired results:** Everything went according to plan, so all you have to do is document what was done for future reference.

2. **Implemented as planned, did not get the desired results:** You took the actions specified in the plan, but the outcome wasn't what you expected. You need to reevaluate the plan—because there is likely either a critical piece of information you overlooked or conditions have changed since you first put out the plan, making the original actions outdated.

3. **Did not implement as planned, got the desired results:** The only reaction to this situation is that you were extremely lucky! Somehow everything worked out well despite people not following the plan. You need to document what was done versus what was planned— perhaps you can save someone else a lot of time in the future.

4. **Did not implement as planned, did not get the desired results:** The question is why the plan wasn't followed—and don't immediately jump to finger-pointing! Instead, look at possible reasons why the plan wasn't followed. Perhaps you did a poor job of educating people about the plan, or you didn't give them adequate instructions, or you didn't prepare them with the right knowledge or skills. Perhaps there were incentives still in place that rewarded people for continuing to act in old ways. Find the underlying reason, correct it, and try again.

To determine which category your implementation falls into, you have to have appropriately documented your work in all the ASPIRE phases leading up to the E phase.

An evaluation process not only involves identifying the right metric types, but it also determines the best means to measure results. Chapter 10 discusses in depth how to measure and monitor progress based on quantitative data and observable results.

Change typically involves both business and behavioral results, which means you have to look beyond sheer numbers to judge overall effectiveness and genuine success. For that reason, a combination of quantitative and qualitative survey research is often necessary to evaluate the behavioral, or soft-side, outcomes. Quantitative surveys assess such factors as the degree of individual commitment to—or participation in—the initiative. Often conducted as a follow-up to quantitative surveys, qualitative studies include "soft soundings" research and focus groups to determine thoughts, attitudes, perceptions, and emotions that may figure into issues of individual engagement.

Doing a Stakeholder Analysis

Having a good understanding of people's attitudes toward the change and preparedness for change is critical to creating an effective change plan. So I want to spend extra time focusing on the A in ASPIRE—how to do an effective stakeholder analysis as part of an assessment.

People in changing organizations work and behave in accordance with their perceptions. So you must make every effort to understand their attitudes and motivations prior to undertaking a business change, especially a large-scale one. Understanding their perceptions allows you to calibrate the likelihood of their engagement at various points during the change.

WHY PEOPLE CHOOSE TO ACT

When you were developing the vision and business case, you may have already started gathering information about the key questions at this stage:

- What are the benefits of this project?
- How will it enable the business to operate more productively?
- What level of change is involved in this effort?
- How does this project impact third parties?
- What worries the third parties about this project?

During the Assess the As-Is phase, you want to expand your efforts and ask these key questions of the project manager, the implementation team, members of support functions (such as IT or HR), and other people or groups important to the change process.

You need to determine the level of understanding by the people most impacted by the change. Having an in-depth profile (discussed below) of the stakeholders involved with and affected by the change will help you develop effective strategies and tactics for engaging them and obtaining their active participation. In addition, it will provide sponsors with the necessary insights to avoid or reduce change resistance and other behavioral or attitudinal expressions that may prove detrimental to the effort.

To prepare a comprehensive stakeholder profile, create four lists:

1. **Stakeholder groups that will be *directly impacted* by the change.** Directly impacted stakeholders are internal constituents whose ways of working will be primarily and/or significantly affected by the proposed change.
2. **Stakeholder groups that will be *indirectly impacted* by the change.** Indirectly impacted stakeholders are internal constituents whose ways of working will be moderately or slightly affected by the proposed change.
3. **Stakeholder groups that will be *adjacently impacted* by the change.** Adjacently impacted stakeholders are internal constituents whose ways of working won't be affected by the proposed change, but who should be aware of it because they support those who will be directly or indirectly impacted.
4. **Stakeholder groups who should be *generally aware* of the change but will not be impacted to any extent.**

For each stakeholder group, document their likely knowledge of the change as well as their perceptions, sensitivities, and/or biases regarding it. Also document considerations that may be useful to keep in mind for the duration of the change process.

Quantitative Surveys vs. Qualitative Reviews

Conducting surveys of representatives from each stakeholder group is one way to determine stakeholder needs. Surveys provide important qualitative information compared to quantitative research, which may come in handy at other points in your project (see Table 5-2).

Qualitative Research	Quantitative Research
Deals in words, images, and the subjective.	Deals in numbers, logic, and the objective.
Recommended during earlier phases of an initiative.	Recommended during latter phases of an initiative.
You may only know somewhat in advance the information you seek.	You know clearly in advance the information you seek.
The design emerges as the survey unfolds.	All aspects of the survey are carefully designed before data is collected.
The moderator gathers the data.	As the change sponsor, you use tools, such as questionnaires or equipment, to collect data. No moderator is involved.
Data is reported in the form of words, pictures, or objects.	Data is reported in the form of numbers and statistics.
Data is considered richer in context and insight, resulting from a time-consuming collection process, and it is less able to be generalized.	Data is more efficient, able to test hypotheses, but it is often lacking in explanatory detail.
Moderator runs risk of becoming subjectively immersed in the subject matter.	You tend to remain objectively separated from the subject matter.

Table 5-2. Comparing qualitative and quantitative research

Assessing the Findings

Now that you're done interviewing key people, you've got pages and pages of notes to organize. Here are two steps to help you compile your data:

1. **Identify common themes.** Often participants employ similar language to similar questions asked of other participants. Language that's aligned among participants often indicates alignment on the underlying subject. Common themes might cover topics such as:

REVIEWING PAST INITIATIVES
One of the best ways to begin your stakeholder analysis is to review past change initiatives. Depending on your organization, you might be able to access information—lessons learned—about previous change projects. These lessons are an invaluable resource for determining how your stakeholders feel about change and what might or might not work for your change.

For instance, you might learn that a previous change initiative ran into difficulty because people weren't trained properly. But why weren't they? Did they not take the training classes? Did they need classroom-style training, but were only offered online training? Did management not put enough value or emphasis on training? Were the training materials insufficient for the degree of training required?

Based on the answers you find, you can incorporate appropriate solutions and tactics into your project. If previously employees weren't taking training, you might establish training as a mandatory activity, assign employees to specific training classes, and require training before an employee can work in the new environment.

Reviewing past initiatives is helpful because past performance is often a good predictor of what an organization will do if left to its own devices.

- Understanding the change's goal
- Past change experiences
- Employee impacts
- Leadership's role and responsibilities
- Cultural issues
- Consensus on benefits

2. **Identify areas where answers conflict.** These answers show you where alignment is needed and how far apart the leaders are on these topics.

Acting on Your Findings

Once you've assessed the data and identified the common and divergent viewpoints, it's time to make your recommendations and take action. Begin by reporting the findings to your sponsor or steering committee. Include recommendations on how to optimize the aligned areas and create alignment in the divergent areas.

Be an Architect of Change

Just as an architect goes through a deliberate process when designing a new building, you must be an architect of change, going through deliberate steps to plan and implement a change effort. Like an architect creating a blueprint for a contractor to follow while building a structure, you need to design a change program that others can implement effectively.

The ASPIRE framework explained in this chapter will help you create a solid plan that makes it clear who does what, when, and why. Change like that will be not only accepted but embraced by those who have to do the changing. You can then take a backseat and let others have the limelight. The better your blueprint, the better the quality of the change implementation.

Manager's Checklist for Chapter 5

- ☑ A change effort must follow a specific sequence of steps so that people won't put the cart before the horse.
- ☑ Your role is like that of an architect: you design the plan or blueprint that others implement.
- ☑ The ASPIRE framework defines the right sequence: Assess the As-Is, Set Standards, Plan Programs, Implement Initiatives, Recognize Results, Evaluate Effectiveness.
- ☑ As the change architect, you are involved in all the ASPIRE steps, but you will only be held accountable for the Plan step.
- ☑ Companies are often tempted to skip the Assessment step, but you shouldn't fall into that trap. Everyone thinks they understand the current state, and they all do—but with different perceptions. You need to document what's really happening before the change effort gets under way so you will be able to do a reasonable assessment of the "after" state. Also, understanding up front what people know (or think they know) about the change effort will help you better decide what to include in your plan.

☑ You need to define goals that specifically describe how the end state will differ from the current state.

☑ Make sure you have methods for evaluating how and how well employees are participating in the change effort. There should be rewards to reinforce positive outcomes, and consequences if people fail to live to up to expectations.

☑ To evaluate the effectiveness of the change effort, be sure you know how you will (1) be able to tell if the plan was implemented as designed, and (2) what the results were.

Creating Awareness

The fish only knows that it lives in the water, after it is already on the river bank. Without our awareness of another world out there, it would never occur to us to change.

—Unknown

When it's time to evaluate the effectiveness of change program strategies, people will always say there could have been more communication. The survey results on why change initiatives fail in Chapter 2 demonstrated the point (see Figure 2-2).

But it takes far more than communication to create change in an organization. There are five strategies that create change: *awareness, understanding, engagement, leverage,* and *measurement.* To varying degrees, all five should be used in every initiative. The first change strategy we are going to discuss is awareness.

For every change effort—and every element in the change effort—there's a first moment when people hear about it, a first impression of what's coming down the pike. That initial communication doesn't create the change, but it does create awareness that *something* is happening. And the attitude people will have toward that "something" is determined by how well you handle the creation of awareness.

Remember the change curve from Chapter 1? As I discussed, the purpose of change management is to reduce the size of the productivity drop-off and lead to a speedier achievement of even higher productivity. The work you do to build awareness starts before the change is introduced, and it helps determine the trajectory of the curve you're trying to influence (Figure 6-1).

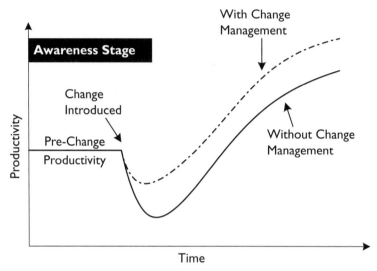

Figure 6-1. Change curve

I think of the goal of "awareness" as analogous to the alarm clock built into my cell phone called Smart Alarm. Smart Alarm plays soothing nature sounds in a slowly increasing volume for a few minutes before the typical jarring alarm sound. It's a pleasant way to wake up. Creating awareness of a change initiative is much the same as the Smart Alarm feature. Smart Alarm begins the process of changing me from being asleep to a full participant in the day by making me aware that the time has come to get out of bed. I haven't actually gotten out of bed yet, but I know what I have to do to complete the change. I still need to implement the other change strategies if I want to keep my job, of course: Reacquaint myself (understand) with my day's obligations, "engage" with a cup of coffee, figure out whom I need to work with during the day (leverage), and update my to-do list (measurement).

You can attack each of the five communication strategies (awareness, understanding, engagement, leverage, measurement) using the ASPIRE model introduced in Chapter 5 (see Figure 6-2). In this case, pay attention to the first three steps (Assess the As-Is, Set Goals, Plan Programs).

Figure 6-2. The ASPIRE process

Assess the As-Is: Where Does Your Audience Stand?

In the ASPIRE framework discussion in the previous chapter, I talked about how to do a broad assessment to evaluate the readiness of the groups affected by or involved in the change effort. When thinking about creating awareness, your assessment goal is narrower. You should look at the communication environment. The context in which your messages are being distributed affects how communication needs to be executed. You need to know the organization's current:

- Business objectives, supporting strategies, and general level of business health.
- Structure and key leaders. Who will be the people issuing communications about the initiative?
- Flow of major organizational activities. Examples include impacts of business seasonality on workload, annual planning cycles, milestones of other major initiatives, enterprise-wide sales meetings, and industry conventions or standards. Any activity that occupies significant audience bandwidth is not worth competing with.

■ Current communication approaches. Is there an intranet? Does everybody have an e-mail address? Are there regularly scheduled town hall sessions? Which leaders like to get in front of the employee base?

■ The organization's history of major change initiatives and the lessons learned about communicating during those initiatives.

SMART

MANAGING

DON'T FORGET ABOUT THIRD PARTIES

Don't forget about third parties. Your suppliers and customers may have a large interest in your change initiative. I've been on several projects where a systems change at the client organization required testing in the supplier or customer system. If the customers or suppliers are large enough, their timelines can force you to change yours. The more lead time you can give them, the better off you are.

These types of topics have a direct and indirect bearing on how you choose to create awareness for one simple reason: the more you know about the environment you're working in, the smarter the choices you'll make in developing your communication plan.

Conducting an Audience Analysis

The next step is to think about *who* will be affected by the change.

■ Who needs to know and who would want to know about this change?

■ What will my leaders want these people to know, do, and feel about this change?

■ How are these people likely to react to the changes?

Collect the obvious and basic facts about your audience, such as employee location, numbers of people, work schedules, and the ability to access e-mail and corporate intranets. This information should be available from project leadership or the human resources department. Like a hunter needs to know where the prey is, you need to know how to reach your audience.

Gather information about the change itself. I track all this information in a spreadsheet called a Change Impact Log. The spreadsheet captures the following information:

■ **Overview of the change,** e.g., Elimination of Buy on Behalf of Role.

■ **Description for each impacted audience.** Using the example above, a more detailed explanation might be: "The elimination of 'Buy on Behalf of' role in the system means admins will no longer be able to create purchase requisitions for managers. Managers will have to create their own purchase requisitions."

- **Impacted audience.** Continuing to use the above example, you would likely list the fact that admins and managers are impacted by this change. When I create an impact log, I would have two lines: one for managers and one for admins.
- **Likely reaction.** In this example, the reaction from admins might be positive, and the reaction from managers would likely be negative.
- **Date of impact.** Describe when the impact takes place.
- **Messages.** In this spreadsheet cell, I describe how I will likely speak about this change. You can treat these notes as preliminary speaking points. Don't worry about making it perfect at this point.

Informal audience analysis comes from ongoing conversations with the people who will be impacted by change. Try continuously weaving a change-related question into every conversation. Here are some examples:

- What went well/not so well about the organization's last change effort?
- How would people describe the organization's culture?
- How would people describe the organization's morale?
- How do people here like to receive information? Written? Town hall sessions?
- How is leadership perceived by most people in the organization?
- What do people already know about the change, and why are we embarking on a change initiative?

Once you have a good understanding of the communications context and the people who will experience the changes, it's time to dig into your analysis more deeply. Your analysis will help you understand the attitudes and knowledge base of those you will be leading through change. Your analysis will help you unlock drivers of WIIFM or What's In It For Me? Knowing somebody's WIIFM helps the change management professional focus his or her efforts efficiently.

Audience analyses are conducted formally and informally. Formal audience analyses are conducted with simple diagnostic tools, such as online surveys, focus groups, and interviews with leaders.

Typical Survey Questions. The questions below can spur your thinking on general questions you might ask in a survey:

1. What level are you within the organization?
   a. First level—I am the CEO or I report to the CEO
   b. Second level—I report to somebody in the first level
   c. Third level—I report to somebody in the second level
   d. Fourth level—I report to somebody in the third level

2. What do you believe are the top two reasons we are implementing this initiative? (pick top two answers):
   a. Provide several choices that enable you to confirm how well people understand the rationale for change. Consider referencing things like cost control, efficiency, productivity, opportunities to build revenue, and competitive pressure.

3. On a scale of 1 to 5, with 5 being "highly compelling" and 1 being "not very compelling at all," please rate your understanding of the rationale for why we are implementing this initiative.
   a. Highly compelling—the case is clear: we need to do this.
   b. It's one of many initiatives, and although important, it's not at the top of the list.
   c. It's something we need to do someday, but maybe not now.
   d. Our current approach is adequate to meet our needs, and I don't understand why we're doing this.
   e. Not at all compelling—this project is ill conceived and should be stopped before we make mistakes.

4. As I look into the next year, I am most worried about the following aspects of the implementation (pick top two answers):
   a. Interruptions to day-to-day operations.
   b. Changes to reporting.
   c. Allocating people and money to the initiative.
   d. Training and my people's ability to operate in the new world.
   e. We have a relatively good model now. I'm worried about changing to something untested.
   f. Taking focus away from more important initiatives.

g. Resistance to change from the employees under me.

h. I'm really not worried. This is hard, but not impossible.

i. Other.

5. As you understand what the company wants from your team over the next year, this project is what number on your priority list? #1, #2, #3, #4, #5?

6. I see the initiative as an opportunity to (pick one):

a. Really think through our business model, change outdated ways of working, and reinvent ourselves.

b. A means to have better data so we make better decisions.

c. Fulfill a request from our parent company—nothing more, nothing less.

d. Confuse ourselves with something that has nothing to do with our biggest challenges.

7. To make the initiative go as smoothly as possible, I would like to see (pick your top two answers):

a. Regular communication from the people in charge of the initiative.

b. Opportunities for my team members to be involved so they aren't overwhelmed at training.

c. Management holding the IT department accountable for its success.

d. Management putting businesspeople in charge of the business decisions on the implementation.

e. A complete plan so I can see how my people are going to be impacted and adequately prepare.

f. A delay in taking this on. We are too busy to work on it this year.

f. Other:

Interviewing Leadership. When dealing with leadership, you may want to do one-on-one interviews instead of a survey. Use the following questions to spur your thinking about what to ask your leadership:

USE ONLINE SURVEYS

TRICKS OF THE TRADE

These days, you needn't bother printing and distributing hard copies of surveys. Running a survey online is easy and either free or inexpensive. Use Google to find the various survey providers. You'll be amazed at how easy it is.

Questions to determine their understanding of the project

1. How do you see this project supporting the organization's broader objectives?
2. What do you hope to gain from the project?
3. What needs to be in place for this to happen? (Probe for barriers/enablers to change.)
4. What about this project keeps you awake at night?
5. What role would you like to play in driving change throughout the organization?

Questions about impacts and communications

1. What areas will be most impacted by the project, and how will your group be impacted?
2. Which people will be most impacted?
3. What is the best way to communicate to the people in your area/function?
4. How would you evaluate the communications to date?

Questions about organizational change

1. How will people in your group react to the changes?
2. What other major initiatives are going on in your team? How might those initiatives impact this project?
3. Can you tell me about your experiences with other large-scale projects? What went well, and what would you hope never happens again?
4. What inherent risks do you see in this project?

These leadership interview questions will start from your impact log, but you'll add a lot of of content to that log at the conclusion of every interview. The informal information you gather will give you great insight into the organization.

Although I'm sure there are valid examples where the following rule doesn't apply, in general, it's hard to *over*assess. The more common problem is *under*-assessing. Don't be limited by the list of assessment areas, and never assume anything. There are valuable lessons to be found on the shop floor where the organization's most basic work is performed. You may even find yourself checking on things like literacy, language skills, and computer skills.

Set the Goals: Establish Your Awareness Goals

Essentially, your awareness goals are what a group needs to *know, do,* or *feel* something specific. You need to determine which of those outcomes you're looking for and expand on them by defining:

- What date ...
- What percent of ...
- Which group of people ...
- To know, do, or feel ...
- What specific message or set of messages

> **BE CONSISTENT!** CAUTION
> When gathering information on a formal basis, be sure to ask the same question of each interviewee. If you ask different questions, or ask them in different ways, you'll have a harder time interpreting the results and establishing a baseline against which to measure progress.

> **THE KEY QUESTION** TRICKS OF THE TRADE
> If you want to know what people think, ask them to describe "how most people think." Nine times out of 10, you'll get *their* thoughts.

For example, a simple goal might be "By May 1, 65 percent of plant employees will have signed up for one after-shift information session."

Remember, you won't move an organization from Point A to Point B through one-way communications. You communicate to generate awareness.

Plan Your Awareness Program: How Will You Communicate?

Communicating about change has some unique attributes to keep in mind. At the top of the list is the fact that the leader is about to ask a group of people to do something they may not want to do. I suggest to you that the execution of your communication is less about the editorial calendar you create and more about the genuine display of high-quality leadership by your executives. As you shape your communication plan, keep in mind the best practices described in Table 6-1.

Crafting the Messages

There are two types of messages in a change initiative. I call them key messages and targeted messages.

SMART

MANAGING

Be Practical in Setting Targets

Never set your awareness goal (or any communication goal, for that matter) at reaching 100 percent of your workforce. First, you only need a critical mass of the people to get *all* of the people moving in a particular direction. Once you get to two-thirds, almost everybody begins to follow the crowd. Second, you'll never get to 100 percent. You'll be amazed at the number of times you'll deliver a message and learn that people are confused because they didn't process all the preceding messages you delivered!

Key messages are the strategic and overarching statements about the initiative that will be repeated over and over throughout the project. Senior management should be communicating these messages consistently. These statements provide the context within which all other messages are crafted. Try to capture your key messages in an elevator pitch.

TRICKS OF THE TRADE

A Brand Name or Logo

Many sponsors like to use a brand name or code name for an initiative. If your organization doesn't have an internal creative services group to help you create a brand identity for your change initiative, it's easy and inexpensive to find those services on the Internet. A little work with Google should quickly find you something. Search on the term *logo design*.

KEY TERM

Elevator pitch A summary statement that can be delivered quickly. Imagine that you wanted to sell your boss on a new project and you're in an elevator with that person. You have only as much time as it takes for the elevator to reach the right floor to explain your idea and gain the executive's support—that's your elevator pitch. Your elevator pitch should be written down and provided to any executive who might be in a position to communicate to others about the project.

Targeted messages are those points relevant to a subset of the group affected by the change. Targeted messages tend to be specific. If you've been diligent in maintaining your impact log, you already have the raw material for your targeted messages.

Throughout most of the Awareness stage, you are primarily crafting key messages focused on making the case for change leading up to the formal announcement of what kind of change is coming (see Figure 6-3). These "we need to change" key messages should address the information you

Best Practices	Definition	Why It's Important
Led by line management	Change strategies should be executed by line management and supported by change management and other support staff.	Employees place their trust and confidence in those they report to. They are inclined to follow those they trust. Hearing about large-scale change from staff functions leads them to believe management may be hiding something.
Consistent with organizational priorities	All change initiatives should be positioned as being part of a larger effort.	Changes consistent with previously understood messages are easier to understand. If the change is truly new, it should be connected with marketplace or environmental dynamics that would be easily understood.
Multidimensional	Messages need to be communicated multiple times through multiple channels.	Some people learn best by hearing, and some learn best by reading. There are lots of competing messages in a workplace. To break through the noise and reach people the way they process information, it's important to repeat, repeat, and repeat some more.

Table 6-1. Communication best practices

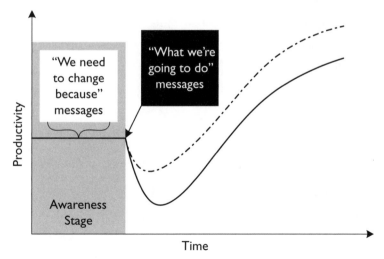

Figure 6-3. Timing of awareness messages

worked through when crafting the vision (see Chapter 3) about why it's necessary for your company to implement the new system, merge with another company, reorganize, relocate, etc. That rationale must be clearly stated and compelling. You'll find yourself repeating it over and over throughout the change process.

Picking the Messenger

A key part of any communication plan is picking the messenger: deciding *who's going to say what*. Studies show that the messenger can be as important to the audience's receptiveness as the message. That's because people identify more easily with people who are like themselves. So choosing the right messenger is critical for successful communication.

First, determine if your message is a key message or a targeted message. Because key messages are broader and more strategic, it usually makes sense for them to come from a management level.

CREATING ANXIETY
Don't be surprised if, unlike my Smart Alarm, your first communication creates anxiety. Your remaining change strategies will reduce the unproductive energy.

However, if your message is targeted to a specific group and topic, you're better off choosing someone more familiar with the targeted audience. The targeted message writer will know:

- How much the audience members already know and what more they need to know
- How much detail they need
- How they feel about the change
- What roles they will perform
- How they will be impacted
- Whom they want to hear from
- What access they have to communication tools

Using the Right Communication Methods

The right communication methods need to be chosen based on the audience, the message, and the messenger. Because we are focusing on the awareness strategy and the "one-way" communication to create aware-

---

PREPARING A "SCRIPT" FOR EXECUTIVES

You might think that an executive doesn't need help knowing what to say when introducing a change effort. In my experience, that's a bad assumption. Executives appreciate people who make their work easier. An executive doesn't have time to create the perfect elevator pitch. You might not get it exactly right, but executives will appreciate that you tried and will work with you to get it right. The executives will be engaged in creating a successful change, and having them participate with you is a big win for the initiative.

---

ness, you will primarily use written vehicles. When we discuss "understanding" in the next chapter, we expand our thinking to dialogue-oriented vehicles. In most organizations, there are a number of potential vehicles for delivering messages. Your As-Is Assessment probably identified:

■ Intranets
■ E-mails and newsletters
■ Corporate announcements
■ Bulletin boards, posters, and video screens

Frequency

If you remember nothing else about communicating to bring about change, remember this: *When it comes to change, there is no such thing as too early or too much communication.* Change initiatives don't fail because communication was overabundant or began too early.

USE EXISTING COMMUNICATION CHANNELS

It's far easier to fit into preestablished communication channels than to create your own. It also means your messages won't compete with other vehicles in the environment. Find the person currently responsible for communicating about organizational initiatives and develop a good relationship with him or her. Also identify the person who helps the field organization communicate with remote personnel. Help from these individuals will be invaluable.

The frequency of your communication depends on three things:

1. Audience
2. Message
3. Degree of anticipated success in reaching the audience

Say, for instance, you're rolling out a new purchasing system for your organization, and you need to notify employees about mandatory training. You might be tempted to think this is a simple, onetime message. But is it really? Not if you want all affected employees to be sure to attend the training (even though it's technically mandatory).

Because the employee is expected to contribute a significant effort regarding training—register for training, attend training, maybe take a test to confirm learning—your communication efforts need to be equally significant. So ensuring that employees participate in training requires multiple communications—"training coming soon," "you need to register for training," "training classes start tomorrow," "don't forget to take your training exam."

Along with frequency comes repetition. Messages seldom hit their target 100 percent the first time. Messages must be repeated through various mediums. In the advertising world, this is called *impressions*. The more impressions a message has, the more likely it is to be heard.

When communicating about change, you must repeat the message multiple times. That doesn't mean you're spamming your audience—messages must be appropriate, timely, etc.—but it does mean you're doing everything you can so your messages have the best shot at reaching their anticipated end point. Even brief mentions in nonrelated areas will reinforce your message.

Creating the Plan Document

Okay. We finally got here. You know the context in which you're going to communicate, you know what information needs to get out, you know whom you need to reach, and you have some awareness goals to achieve. You also have some best practices to keep in mind as you work. It's time to create your communication plan.

Communication plans come in many shapes and sizes. I have seen 50-page presentations to describe the plan. I have also seen simple spreadsheets that function more as an editorial calendar. Your plan should be built to meet both your needs and management's needs. I typically find myself explaining my plan in a short presentation and then working daily from a spreadsheet.

Your management would likely expect the following elements in a communication plan presentation:

Situation Summary. Provide your understanding of the changes that will occur and the assumptions you have crafted in light of your audience analysis.

Plan Summary. Provide an overview of the objectives you want to achieve, who will communicate (the messengers), the messages, the vehicles you will use (methods), and the timelines. Also, provide the guiding principles or best practices that you will follow.

How the Plan Will Work. Discuss how you will make the plan operational. Provide information about roles and responsibilities, and the processes to be followed (such as content approval).

Next Steps. Identify the actions that each stakeholder must take to make the plan operational.

Your detailed plan (the editorial calendar spreadsheet) would likely contain the following columns:

- Communication vehicle or activity
- Timing
- Target audience
- Objectives
- Messenger
- Responsible party
- Status

Implementing, Recognizing, and Evaluating

Let's return to the architect analogy. At this point, you've assessed the building site, understood the owner's intent, and developed a great set of blueprints. The architect must now hand those blueprints over to the construction crew. The architect's role changes now. He or she will continue to provide detail, but much of the work happens "in the trenches" now. A change management professional can write the material, but ultimately, the leader has to deliver it.

Your job at this phase should focus on the following areas:

- Delivering timely materials for use by management
- Recognizing and thanking those members of management who excel at communication
- Listening to the workforce so you can continuously evolve and build on your communication plan

TRICKS OF THE TRADE

TRACK YOUR KEY MESSAGES

Although it will be difficult to track all the targeted messages delivered by every manager, you should track the delivery of key messages by the executive leadership. Tracking should include evaluating those communications planned versus those delivered. You will need this information during your evaluation of the completed change effort.

The Critical Awareness Step

There are a lot of factors that can make a change team want to move fast. There should be a good business case for change—meaning completing the change is important, and the sooner begun, the sooner finished. The change team is naturally eager to see their effort come to fruition. That can lead them to shortchange the Awareness phase. Don't fall into that trap. Take the time to clearly communicate the need for change and to craft the best way to announce exactly what's going to change. This is critical for determining which of the change curves on Figure 6-1 you'll follow. Handle these first steps wrong, and you can see a steep drop in productivity and a long recovery period. Handle it correctly, and the drop won't be so deep. You'll also see a rebound to higher productivity faster because people will be more committed to making the change.

The other trap to avoid is thinking that awareness is a one-and-done strategy in a change effort. Far from it. You'll need to include an awareness strategy as each element of your vision and plan is put into place.

Manager's Checklist for Chapter 6

☑ Awareness is the first of five strategies to use when implementing any aspect of a change.

✓ The early communication has two components: The first is to make the case for change (We need to change because . . .). The second is to describe the change itself (So we're going to . . .).

✓ Use the ASPIRE process to develop and implement your awareness strategy.

✓ To shape the best awareness messages, you must understand the current state of your business and your audiences' attitudes about the current state. Figure out who needs to know what, and what the leaders of those people must know, do, or feel.

✓ Conduct employee surveys and interview leaders to gather information about attitudes.

✓ Gather quantitative information about past changes so you know what worked and what didn't.

✓ Determine your goals and develop plans accordingly.

✓ Think carefully about who should deliver what messages.

✓ Use existing communication channels as much as possible.

Ensuring
Understanding

It is understanding that gives us an ability to have peace. When we understand the other fellow's viewpoint, and he understands ours, then we can sit down and work out our differences.

—Harry S. Truman

In the midst of a major transformation initiative, employees often surprise senior managers with their responses to open-ended survey questions. Instead of encouraging leaders to discontinue the use of surveys or focus only on the positive results, I am a big fan of ensuring senior management is aware of all comments and responds visibly and appropriately.

A client in the midst of a reorganization retained my company to direct the change management aspects of its initiative. The 7,000-employee business was moving from a single corporate entity to a divisional structure along product lines. These moves were not expected to reduce head count except for a few senior-level positions. The economy was healthy, and this company had been meeting its objectives when the change began.

Senior management had been thinking that a reshuffling of the chairs shouldn't create too much concern with the workforce. They were surprised when employees gave the following input in an anonymous survey:

- It appears we are doing a lot of explaining without a lot of information being revealed. Rumors, speculation, and anxiety grow while we wait. I would have done more "behind the scenes" work and made the changes less visible to the organization until we were ready to make the change.

- I would like to see more "personal" meetings with senior levels. Although the communications are effective, they speak to a broad audience. I would like to see members of the executive team go to each site and personally speak to smaller groups of people to explain the rationale and changes.

- The communications have improved from senior management. There should be weekly bulletins.

- Be open and honest. The rumor mill is rampant about 20 percent headcount reductions. The change was not communicated this way in the beginning. There is even less communication now than ever. Associates want to know the dates when they will find out about their destinies. The vision about accelerated growth has disappeared. There is next-to-no communication about process changes except to those directly involved.

- Set an exact timetable. We keep hearing conflicting dates.

- My manager has done an abysmal job of explaining this to our group, has shown no compassion, and seems disinterested in our concerns. The process is too slow and is killing our culture. We hear very little from the executives and they don't do any "walking around."

- Will these moves really change the company and break down silos? Or is it really a financial restructuring that will enable us to sell off parts of the company?

What can you take away from these comments beyond the fact that rumors fill vacuums? The group responding to this survey was clearly aware of the changes but had conflicting understandings of what those changes meant. The organization clearly was struggling with change.

In the previous chapter, we discussed how to make employees aware. In this chapter, we discuss how to take awareness a step further—to foster understanding.

Poised for Success

Wouldn't it be great if all you had to do to create a change was build awareness? Change would be easy. But awareness isn't enough. You must also foster understanding—which ultimately leads to participation.

CONTEXT CREATES COMFORT

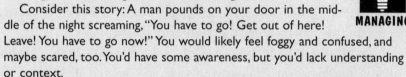

SMART MANAGING

Without understanding, employees feel lost and insecure. Understanding evolves through context and dialogue.

Consider this story: A man pounds on your door in the middle of the night screaming, "You have to go! Get out of here! Leave! You have to go now!" You would likely feel foggy and confused, and maybe scared, too. You'd have some awareness, but you'd lack understanding or context.

Let's say instead this same man pounds on your door, but in addition to his insistence that you leave your home, he provides context: "The home next to yours is on fire, and it's starting to spread to the roof of your house!"

In one situation, you have a bit of awareness about the situation, but no understanding. In the second situation, you have context and understanding to help you make the decision about whether you should call the police or thank the man for saving your life. Once you understand, you can take informed action.

In the situation that opened this chapter, the context that drove the reorganization was the company's decision to move away from being constrained by country borders and to move toward a global structure organized by product groups. With that context, employees could begin to understand how and why the company was changing.

How do we build understanding? Think back to Chapter 6 as it pertains to building awareness throughout the phases of change. We discussed messages, audiences, methods, and frequency—and used the WIIFM (What's In It For Me) principle. But we did so in a generic sense.

Now, we're going to build understanding by involving more than people's ears. In fact, I like to categorize these three change strategies like this:

- Awareness = Head
- Understanding = Heart
- Participation = Hands

Awareness requires only one-way communication—directed at the recipients. In a change project, awareness is created when you inform employees of the change and what will happen. Intellectually, they hear the message in their *heads.* When you are in the role of the change leader, you can accomplish awareness by talking *to* employees.

Understanding, though, requires two-way, shared communication—wherein the recipients spread information to others and provide feedback. Intuitively, they feel the message in their *hearts.* When you're in the role of change leader, you cement understanding by talking *with* employees and encouraging them to continue the conversation with others.

Ultimately, this increased level of awareness and understanding results in participation (which we discuss in Chapter 8). In time, the recipients act out the message with their *actions.*

Creating awareness is easy, and it doesn't take much time. Fostering understanding, however, requires more time—but significantly increases people's ability to change in the right direction (see Figure 7-1).

> **SMART MANAGING**
>
> ## UNDERSTANDING IS TWO-WAY
>
> As Eleanor Roosevelt once said, "Understanding is a two-way street." You don't build understanding by talking *at* or *to* people. You build understanding by empowering people to talk *with* others.

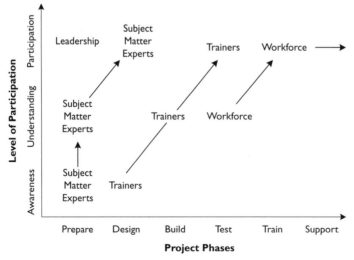

Figure 7-1. An organization in change

Cascading Information

Understanding occurs best through two-way exchanges of information. The exchange of information in a change project is pretty simple, and it contains two main elements:

1. Cascading dialogue through all levels of management
2. Training the workforce in the new way of working

I will expand on this shortly, but first consider this system implementation project. Like many systems projects, it has six phases, as outlined in Figure 7-1:

1. **Prepare.** Leadership organizes the project, provides clear objectives, and assembles a project team with resources—and authority—to get the job done.
2. **Design the future.** The project team determines the future state and designs the change.
3. **Build it.** The team builds the new system.
4. **Test it.** Before going live with the new system, the team tests it thoroughly.
5. **Train it.** Employees receive training to be successful in the new world.
6. **Support.** Support plans are put in place to help people work in the new system.

Throughout these phases, awareness and understanding need to be fostered across the whole organization, and we can make some assumptions about how this understanding develops:

NONSYSTEMS CHANGES HAVE SIMILAR PHASES **SMART MANAGING**
Even if your project isn't systems related, it will have these same six phases. I worked on an office relocation effort once within a company whose headquarters was moving 30 miles away. We followed the same general flow.

- Senior leadership usually has a pretty good understanding of what a new system entails. They may not understand all the details—but they will "get" the big pieces.
- A team will begin working on the project, gaining understanding as they go. The project team will ultimately have the most detailed understanding of the "to-be" state.

TRICKS OF THE TRADE

COMMUNICATE ABOUT REWARDS

Some companies fail to communicate about what matters in a way that matters. World at Work's "Sales Compensation Practices 2008" report, a survey of more than 400 compensation and human resources managers, tells the story as it pertains to salespeople in an organization. According to the study, 76 percent of companies change their sales compensation plans every year. This wasn't a surprise to me. Additionally:

- 58 percent of these organizations communicate these changes directly to frontline sales managers.
- 14 percent communicate directly to the sales force.
- 13 percent take a decentralized approach.
- 7 percent do nothing.

These findings mean that 42 percent of companies don't communicate these changes directly to frontline sales managers! Think about that. Assuming that changes in compensation plans are designed to motivate the sales force, how effective is *no awareness and no understanding* going to be on motivating for more sales? Obviously, it's not.

I share the following thought, not as a change management practitioner, but as a former salesperson and sales manager: Salespeople—and people in general—are reward driven. Make sure your people understand what your organization wants from them. If they understand, you might get what you want. If they don't understand, you are counting on getting lucky.

- Once the members of the project team understand the details, they will help the managers and trainers understand.
- Once the trainers understand, the workforce can understand.

Naturally, cascading between leadership and employees occurs among various levels at different times. Senior leaders gain awareness and understanding of the strategic changes before frontline employees. Frontline employees may learn of new information received during the test phase before senior leaders. But for now, we've laid out a solid idea of who is communicating and about what. Let's keep drilling down.

Your goal is to engage the various groups to dialogue constructively. When leaders and managers dialogue, both groups walk away with a greater understanding of how to fine-tune the plan in real time.

Engaging Senior Leaders in Understanding

Often, confusion abounds about the impacts of a change. Dialogue is crucial to combating confusion and creating alignment. As the change leader, you live and breathe the change, but others are not as close to it. You may already have forgotten more than others have yet to understand. To preempt confusion and foster understanding at all levels, your job is to initiate dialogue between leadership (top level) and management (middle level).

ON HOLIDAY

I worked on a project that was due to roll out on a global basis at the end of September. I learned through some conversations with various managers and trainers, however, that no one from the European business units could develop training materials during August. Those units were on holiday, and they weren't about to change plans for the project. My team changed plans to accommodate this conflict. We found a solution because the dialogue went both ways.

Throughout the project, you must ensure that leaders and managers are having a dialogue about:

- What the workforce needs to know and when they need to know it
- The questions the workforce might have and how you will answer them

AVOIDING CONFLICT AMONG TEAMS

In one project I worked on, one of the big "aha moments" arose because we got people talking about the intersection of the project's key activities with the key activities in other parts of the business. The management in one part of the business thought it was a good idea to shut down production in July to implement new tooling since it would coordinate with a week when customers were on shutdown. What this group didn't realize was that the new tooling team would also need to work on the new system implementation. Tooling and systems were in conflict. The dialogue helped these groups understand each party's perspectives and priorities and rework the plan accordingly.

Don't assume that constructive dialogue will happen on its own. Instead, ensure that leadership and management levels gain the appropriate level of understanding by engineering the dialogue. In effect, as the change manager you are the dialogue facilitator and driver. Get people talking. Force the talking to happen on a schedule.

I've driven dialogue among senior leadership by structuring a dia-

CONNECTING THE DOTS

One of the biggest reasons important conversations don't happen is that people are afraid of not knowing the answers. No one wants to open a black hole. Essentially, one of your tasks is to help people understand that it's okay not to have all the answers.

Set the tone for dialogue early in the project, and you will encourage people to collaborate in exploring the questions and finding answers. In effect, you play matchmaker between the mind of one person and another to fill in the gaps of content. While one person might not have the answers, another will—and those answers dissipate fear and build confidence. You set the stage for understanding by facilitating dialogue about concerns and solutions. You help connect people and their ideas—also connecting the dots among various elements of your change initiative.

KEY TERM **Impact session** This is a meeting between leadership and management to discuss the impact of a major change.

logue specifically about the impacts of the change. It did not require much creativity to name these meetings "impact sessions."

Key Elements of an Impact Session

While building understanding at your impact sessions, answer the following questions:

- What is the company doing?
- Why is it doing it?
- What's in it for each stakeholder (value proposition)?
- What do you want each employee to know, do, or feel as a result of every conversation you have?
- What can your employees do to support this change?

The answers to these questions are as essential to management engagement as an "elevator speech" is for a potential job candidate to get a job interview.

Early in your change initiative, impact sessions should cover business performance and drivers. A discussion of business performance sets the stage for change. For example, discuss:

The Business Reason for Change

- How is the business performing—where is the business today versus where it needs to be?
- What business issues or drivers are making change necessary?
- Why do we need to change now?
- What are the risks to the business of not changing?

Once the rationale has been set, you can move to the meat of the discussion.

The Change Being Implemented

- What has been decided?
- What hasn't been decided yet?
- How does the change answer the business issues that were previously discussed?

THE PROGRESSION OF DIALOGUE   SMART

MANAGING

The dialogue keeps moving along with the project. The business reasons for change are relevant at the project start. As you progress through the project, the conversation changes. As the story of your change works down through the organization, it also moves into greater specificity. In the design phase, you may talk about a new process. In the build phase, you might discuss how training will be scheduled and coordinated. You drive the leaders and managers to talk about what comes next.

How Can We Personally Navigate the Changes?

An effective impact session is one wherein people are encouraged to ask questions like:

- What will the change mean to me?
- What will happen to me if we don't change?
- What are the benefits to me of changing?

For example, if you were in a buggy whip company in the early 1900s, you might hold an impact session to discuss the declining need for buggy whips. The business impact might be that the company would either be forced out of business or would need to adapt. Similarly, on a personal level, the personal impact might be that the whip engineers would be struggling with what it means to change oil in a car.

CONSPIRACY?

CAUTION A friend has a quote: "Never assume there is a conspiracy. The simpler answer of 'stupidity' is usually the right one." There is a corollary in change management: "Never underestimate the potential for people to be unaware, misunderstand, misinterpret, or forget that which you have gone through numerous times. It goes with the territory." The lesson in this is that ongoing dialogue is crucial—to keep people clear on what is occurring.

TIPS FOR PLANNING AN EFFECTIVE IMPACT SESSION

TRICKS OF THE TRADE
1. Make your sessions structured and scheduled. Managers are busy and don't want to waste time with unnecessarily disorganized or last-minute meetings.
2. Build in accountability and enticement for managers to report key discoveries to their departments. For example, you can survey departments to find out what they are hearing and learning from their managers.
   ■ When survey findings tell you that a manager is doing an outstanding job communicating to her people, thank her. Then send a quick note to her manager reporting her great work.
   ■ When survey findings show you that a gap exists, share the survey results with the manager and ask what you can do to help make sure that essential information gets to the right level of employees.
3. To be successful, equip the presenters with "meetings in a box." These might consist of "canned" presentations, speaking points, Q&As, wall visuals, etc. In other words, make it easy for the presenters to look good, be prepared, and deliver successful presentations.
4. Always assign a person to be responsible for documenting the meeting and helping the facilitator if needed.

Understanding the Story Behind the Change

Many organizations err by focusing only on the facts and figures of a change message as if a "data dump" is the best catalyst for action. Consider a company going through a huge change, like a merger between giants. The merger is costly and risky, but leaders from both companies determine that the merger must take place as a matter of survival. In this case, a story such as the one below might set the tone for the employees better than a spreadsheet alone:

In 1988, a fire broke out on an oil-drilling platform off the coast of Scotland. More than 160 crew members and rescuers died that night, but a superintendent of the rig, Andy Mochan, survived. From his hospital bed, Mochan described jumping 150 feet off the fiery platform into the icy sea below, and he explained his decision by saying: "It was either jump or fry." He chose possible death over certain death (source: www.mentoric.com/resource_wall_of_fire.html).

In many organizations, this real story has come to be known as the "burning platform" metaphor. In other words, will the organization remain on a burning platform, or will people do something about it?

Just as Mochan could easily explain why he jumped, you should easily be able to answer the question, "Why change?" Your answer might be something like this: "If we fail to (insert merger rationales here), both companies will close our doors—maybe not today or tomorrow, but we will become insolvent within the next few years. We are going to merge to secure our best chance of long-term survival."

> **STORIES GET STUCK** **SMART MANAGING**
>
> Speaker, consultant, and author of *A Manager's Guide to Employee Engagement* Scott Carbonara (McGraw-Hill, 2013) offers a short reminder on the power of storytelling in conducting impact planning or training: *over time, facts get forgotten; stories get stuck.* While facts provide the intellectual, cognitive level of understanding, stories connect with people on a visceral, emotional level. Many change initiatives create strong feelings, and stories do a better job shaping feelings than facts alone.

Or, in the buggy whip example, you might say, "If we don't stop making buggy whips and start learning to change oil, our company will literally be unnecessary in a few years. We need to produce new products or services to survive this technological change." A story can make the reasons behind the change obvious. Paint a picture to cement understanding.

> **SAMPLE INVITATION TO AN IMPACT SESSION CONVERSATION BETWEEN LEADERSHIP AND MANAGERS**
>
> The rumors are true. The XYZ Project will mean a significant amount of change for the business and our associates, suppliers, and customers. Those changes will begin to impact us in the coming months, and as managers in the business, we want to provide you with the information and tools to

help you effectively lead during this time of change.

As part of our program to ensure we are ready, the Change Team will take several actions. To keep you aware what is occurring, we will regularly send you written material. In fact, the first Change Overview Brief was sent to you last week. We will also be conducting face-to-face sessions on a regular basis. During these sessions we will provide you with information to understand:

- How the XYZ Project fits within the overall transformation of our organization, and how the initiatives fit together.
- How the XYZ Project Change will impact the business, customers, suppliers, and associates. For example, did you know that approximately 2,000 associates will be attending end-user training during the months of November and December?
- How you can help the organization become ready for XYZ. Did you know XYZ will mean changes in how associates do their jobs?
- How to address any resistance you might encounter during this time of transition. Are you ready should it happen on your team?
- How to demonstrate ownership of this vital business initiative—and help team members do the same. For example, what happens when the project ends? Are you prepared to sustain the new way of working?

You are invited to participate in the first of our XYZ Impact Session in the Meeting Room on June X, 20XX at 10 a.m.

Answers to Questions You May Have

1. With so many competing priorities, why should I attend the Impact Sessions?
   We understand that most leaders are under tremendous pressure and adding another meeting to the calendar is difficult, but you have our promise that the material is relevant and timely.

2. May I send a delegate to the meeting?
   We suggest that you don't delegate attendance at this meeting. In times of change, best practices dictate that leaders be on the front lines, and it is hard to demonstrate leadership if you don't understand your role in the change or the specific business impacts of a project of this size. If you do have a conflict that can't be changed, please notify us in advance by sending an e-mail to changeteam@company.com.

3. Who is invited to this meeting?
   All directors at this location have been invited.

Training as the Key to Understanding

Now that the design has been created, built, and tested, you must educate the workforce. You can't expect employees to be engaged in a change or participate fully until they know how it works. While context is key to providing understanding, gaining context often requires training. Each

THE ALLURE OF FOOD — SMART

MANAGING

If you want people to come to a meeting, the solution is simple: provide food. No matter the client, industry, culture, or project, meeting attendance suffers even when attendees are invited to "an important meeting to discuss the future of our business." Something pressing always keeps people away. Offer food, however, and people will consider it multitasking. Feed them and they will come. Make sure you obtain a budget for food.

employee affected by the change must attend training to be proficient in the new way of working.

Depending on the type of project you are involved in, your "training" might be informal—such as explaining how a new organization structure will work. Lunch-and-learn sessions are perfect for this type of material. Alternatively, the training might be a formal program where new skills are taught.

Let's talk about the basics of training, including adult learning theory, learning styles, and developing a training program using ASPIRE.

Lunch-and-Learn An informal educational session occurring over lunch. Often, these are optional — KEY TERMS programs meant to enrich employees, or provide learning to expand their knowledge base.

Training The transfer of a specific skill or skill set from one person to another through formal instruction.

Target the Three Learning Styles

Create two-way dialogue and shared discussion—particularly as it pertains to training—by tapping into people's unique learning styles. In the same way that strong leaders have leadership styles, learners process and retain information in one of three different learning styles: auditory, visual, or kinesthetic. In many cases, people learn best through a combination of the three. Change agents must be proficient in all three learning

ASSIGN SKILLED TRAINERS AND ALLOT ENOUGH TIME

TRICKS OF THE TRADE

Follow these two tips for successful training:

1. Assign someone with the right skills and experience to supervise your training program. An expert can tell you what kind of material should be taught online versus via instructor, and can also tell you how long it will take to train on a given body of work.

   If you aren't a training expert, it is easy to postpone the development of training materials for a day … then two days, then three days. Very soon, you become too far behind to catch up, and you introduce significant risk into your project. Make sure you assign people with the right skills to do the training.

2. Never underestimate the amount of administration it takes to schedule or secure classes, classrooms, training equipment, trainers, materials, and employees. Between the varying needs of managers and employees, business issues, and vacation schedules, what looks simple is actually complex. Put somebody sharp on the task, and let this person ask lots of questions.

CAUTION

MANAGERS NEED TRAINING, TOO

Managers may initially say, "I don't need training on that work. My people do it, not me." They are right—managers usually don't perform the work that their subordinates perform. But I will let you in on a secret that managers will soon figure out: If the manager's employees learn how to perform their jobs from trainers and receive peer-to-peer support from super users, those same people may eventually ask the manager, "Exactly how do you help me do my job? What value do you add?" Managers will realize that if they don't know what their people do every day, their management really isn't needed. If you as a manager get in front of this concept and stay "in the know" about what your employees are learning, you'll be able to look at the upcoming changes without fear of becoming redundant.

styles to reach each employee. Trainers and educators also need to be versed in the learning styles.

Auditory learners process and retain information with their *ears*, both by hearing instructions given by others and by hearing themselves repeat the information back. Auditory learners process through dialogue. For that reason, auditory learners may struggle to absorb information sent using a static, one-way channel—such as reading a how-to manual. Since auditory learners listen to information and repeat it back as a way to cement it clearly in their own minds, they often learn best in a quiet environment that is as distraction free as possible.

Visual learners process and retain information using their *eyes*, so the best way to reach them is by providing graphics like flow charts, learning maps, and uncluttered PowerPoint slides, reading materials, or demonstrations. Visual learners are quick to process symbols and information provided in a linear fashion, but they may get overwhelmed by learning materials that are too "busy" or contain too many key concepts.

Kinesthetic learners process and retain information using their *hands*, meaning they are hands-on and learn best by doing. They might use their ears and eyes to gain awareness, but true kinesthetic learners may get frustrated with too many lectures or demonstrations.

Leverage Adult Learning Theory

For your training to be effective, it should leverage adult learning theory. Engagement and change management author Scott Carbonara uses the acronym E.D.U.C.A.T.O.R. as a mnemonic device for trainers and peer coaches to best engage adult learners. Smart instructional designers consider this set of best practices in development planning by anticipating how adults absorb new information as well as how they will apply that learning back on the job.

Engage their egos
Deliver ongoing feedback
Use context *and* concrete practice
Create social learning
Applaud autonomy
Tie goals to daily activities
Offer ongoing coaching
Respect their expertise

Engage egos. Adults carry around quite a bit of fear when placed in new learning situations. They might fear failing, fear embarrassment of being singled out, or even fear having to speak up in front of others. The best training environment is one where adult learners receive support and guidance from each other to minimize feelings of inadequacy or judgment during learning.

Deliver feedback. When you're driving down the road, you see speed limit signs to tell you the standard established by the local municipality. That's relevant information, but what makes it meaningful is your speedometer, which tells you precisely how fast you are driving. Your speedometer is your feedback channel to keep you within the standard. Likewise, adults need regular feedback about their performance. Ensure that you build in mechanisms that allow learners to hear how they are doing and receive both positive as well as gentle, corrective feedback.

Use context with concrete practice. Teenagers around the world take a course to prepare them for driving a vehicle. These classes are both academic, like driver's education done in the classroom with a pen and paper, and hands-on, like driver's training done behind the wheel of a car on the open road. Similarly, adult learners need both theory (a head level of understanding) and practice (a hands level of understanding) to apply what they learn successfully on the job.

Create social spaces. Back when most of us went to school, working with classmates on an assignment was considered cheating. Lose that mindset. Adults learn best when they participate in small-group discussions and activities to reinforce the learning. This takes them beyond awareness and understanding, and moves them into proficiency. Encourage team efforts as a way for each person to reflect on his or her experiences and share mastery with others.

Applaud autonomy. The Montessori approach to education works well with many learners because it offers a freedom to learn and explore within certain limits, while respecting each learner's unique interest, needs, and style. Adult learners function best when they are given a level of autonomy over what and how they learn.

Tie goals to daily activities. No one is passionate about excelling in busywork. Success in the real world is less about memorizing and reciting a list of facts than it is about achieving goals and objectives that are meaningful to one's role. Make sure what you teach people is directly relevant to what translates to success in their day-to-day activities, helping them to be more proficient or efficient in their roles.

Offer ongoing coaching. People can soak up only so much in the classroom or out on the floor. Don't assume that just because every essential topic got covered in class that every essential topic got *absorbed by every person in the class!* For some learners, the transfer of learning takes more time, or one-on-one coaching is required to make learning stick. Provide this support to adult learners so they can maximize what they learn and convert it into sustainable results.

Respect their expertise. Adult learners may come to you as novices in a new topic, but they are highly competent and educated in a wide range of disciplines, experiences, knowledge, passions, and competencies. If you keep this in mind as part of the professional development planning process, learners will feel valued and respected—two feelings essential to making learners willing to put on their thinking caps and acquire new skills.

> **TRAINING TAKES TIME** SMART
>
> It's estimated that it takes 20 to 35 hours of instructional design to create one hour of training. Preparing training takes a lot of work to do well. Plan accordingly.
>
> MANAGING

Creating a Successful Training Program

Let's get into the how-tos of training. You or the training program managers should execute the following steps to build and deliver your training according to the ASPIRE model:

1. Assess the As-Is: Conduct a Training Needs Analysis

One of the most critical parts of any change plan is staff training so they will be set up to succeed *after* the change has been implemented. Therefore, include a training needs analysis in your plan. Evaluate what knowledge and skills employees need and what training approaches will best achieve those educational goals. Determine what employees already know (the as-is) versus what they need to know (the goals). The difference between these two comprises the objectives of your training program—the gulf between the two states that your training must address.

2. Set Standards: Establish Learning Goals

Here's a sample list of goals for your training program:

- The workforce will be tested and certified for working in the post-change environment, including meeting all learning objectives.
- The project steering committee will review all training materials before delivery.
- All legacy training materials will be identified with a plan in place to archive those materials and remove them from public view.
- The workforce will provide a strongly positive assessment of the quality of the training program.

3. Plan Programs: Plan Your Training

Before you roll out the training, detail the training model. How will it be administered and measured? Will it be through an LMS (learning management system) or in-person training?

LMS (Learning Management Systems) An LMS is "a software application for the administration, documentation, tracking, and reporting of training programs, classroom and online events, e-learning programs, and training content," according to Wikipedia.

KEY TERM

Managers, contact your HR or OD department to find out if your company uses one, because you can leverage the tool for training administration and the storage of computer-based training materials.

To plan an effective training program, define the what, when, who, and how of the training.

4. Implement Initiatives: Conduct Training

Here are some tips to ensure that your training is of high quality. Implement:

- **Accountability for training.** Assign a group or steering committee to be responsible for assessing the quality of the training materials and deciding whether to certify that employees are ready to perform in the new environment.
- **Role-based training.** Training should be based on jobs that employees perform, not necessarily on employee title or position.
- **Progressive delivery/just-in-time training.** Training should be provided in a progressive/just-in-time fashion—meaning that it should be about work people are about to deliver. This will ensure that all trainees retain what they have just learned.

THE BENEFITS OF VIDEO

When planning your education program, consider capturing some of the key sessions to video. You will gain the following benefits:

- Attendance at training will not be 100 percent. Videos give people a chance to catch up on their own schedule.
- People learn in multiple ways. Some people don't process written material well. They need to hear it.
- People often mishear. Videos provide a record.
- People are accustomed to looking at videos. They are easy to process and apply.
- Video production technology is getting easier. Many online learning modalities exist to make distribution a cinch.

■ **Support materials/job aids.** Create a centralized information bank stored in an accessible location, such as in the corporate HR department.

5. Recognize Results

Recognize people for completing their training. I've seen charts put up in breakrooms indicating which employees had attended which classes. I've also seen stickers put on hard hats, small flags put on desks, certificates presented to people, continuing education credits given, and HR files

INVOLVE HR   SMART

Different forms of recognition work differently depending on the place and culture. What works well in one location may not well work well in another. Workplace rules may govern how you recognize achievement. Consult HR as you develop appropriate recognition programs.

MANAGING

updated. Find creative ways to tell people that the fact they attended training was appreciated and that they did a good job.

6. Evaluate Effectiveness. Conduct Post-Training Assessments

After you have delivered the training, assess its success. I recommend using Kirkpatrick Learning Assessments—Level I and II assessments (www.kirkpatrickpartners.com/OurPhilosophy/tabid/66/Default.aspx).

According to Kirkpatrick, these two levels of his evaluation model evaluate:

Level 1: Reaction. "To what degree participants react favorably to the training."

Level 2: Learning. "To what degree participants acquire the intended knowledge, skills, attitudes, confidence, and commitment based on their participation in a training event." The greatest need is to verify by testing that the learner actually met the learning objectives identified in the planning phase.

As mentioned in the previous chapter, providing *awareness* is a relatively easy, straightforward task. But as you can see from this chapter, to facilitate *understanding* requires planning, discipline, and expertise. The tips and tools in this chapter provide you with the best practices to enable understanding for your change initiative. If you use them, your leaders, managers, trainers, and employees will be one step closer to helping each group better *participate* in the change initiative.

 **WERE THE LEARNING OBJECTIVES MET?** The biggest need in post-training assessments is to verify by testing that the employees actually met the learning objectives identified in the planning phase. This ensures that your training was successful in preparing the workforce to operate post-change.

Manager's Checklist for Chapter 7

☑ Building awareness involves one-way communication. Creating understanding requires two-way communication. Both are crucial in a change project.

☑ Understanding is created through dialogue and cascading information throughout the levels of leadership, management, and the workforce.

☑ Communicate about what matters to people, particularly regarding rewards.

☑ Training is necessary to teach people specific skills and transfer broader information. Use the ASPIRE model to plan, implement, and measure the training.

☑ Leverage the three main learning styles and adult learning theory to best reach people in your training.

Participating in the Change Process

A leader is best when people barely know he exists, when his work is done, his aim fulfilled, they will say: we did it ourselves.

—Lao Tzu, *Tao Te Ching*

I worked with a global company in reimplementing a system to track all their projects and the activities of approximately 1,500 employees. Under the previous leader, no one in the company had been consulted on the new system design, and no one had received proper training in how to work with the new setup. As a result, the new system only brought increased problems for this organization. Even worse, the results from the new system weren't satisfactory, let alone stellar, to management.

The woman who called me into the project had been living with the problems created by the first implementation and had complained to her manager. What happens to people who complain? They are frequently put in charge of fixing the situation! As a result, the prior leader was removed, and my client—let's call her Mary—was asked to fix the design of numerous business processes and reconfigure the system to match the redesigned processes.

Some day Mary will view this project as a tremendous opportunity, but she probably doesn't today. In fact, Mary's first approach brought her close to making the same mistakes as her predecessor:

- She started deciding unilaterally how to implement the new system.
- She felt it more important to go quickly than to involve others.
- She tried to solve the problem without engaging the expertise and passion of her entire team.

The only person participating in the project was Mary. She didn't have the strength of a team behind her.

Dwight Eisenhower called leadership "the art of getting someone else to do something you want done because he wants to do it." The quote opening this chapter expresses a similar sentiment: stepping out of the way so people can and will take ownership of their results. These philosophies pave a smarter path to the one my client almost chose. That is, the path that ignites *participation*—engaging members of the workforce to become part of the change rather than people who need to be changed.

SMART

MANAGING

PARTICIPATION VERSUS ENGAGEMENT

You likely have heard the term *employee engagement* as a means of ensuring employees give of their discretionary effort in the workplace. I don't wish to downplay the importance of engagement, but I've instead chosen to use the word *participation*. When I mention *engagement* in my consulting practice, many managers assume they need to invest in expensive engagement surveys and assessments from a consulting firm that specializes in this work. When I talk about *participation*, however, I want you to think of something simpler. I want you to envision lots of people participating in the effort—and doing so in an engaged manner.

Why Participation Is Crucial

Participation drives a successful change endeavor for the following reasons:

Participation fosters a sense of accountability and ownership. The people who help construct the solution have a stronger interest in making it work than those who are merely bystanders or drones doing what they are told. Why? Because the solution *isn't something imposed on them*; the solution *is something they created*. If it fails, it will reflect poorly on them. If it succeeds, it will make them look like rock stars. They have skin in the game in the form of their own reputations.

Participation reduces conflict. As the saying goes, "Keep your friends close and your enemies closer." If you involve employees in the change initiative, you develop a firsthand view into potential problem areas and can manage toward positive outcomes before conflict arises.

Participation creates sustainable change. Structured participation enables sustainable change because all employees and leaders are "in the know" about the desired outcome and the process by which it was achieved. Knowledge is deeper and broader—and liable to become more deeply embedded in the organization.

This chapter is about fostering participation so that your change initiative runs more effectively and is sustainable. Doing so will make your work as a change leader harder at the project's start, but easier during the toughest part of the project, and more sustainable over the long term.

DON'T CONFUSE STRATEGIES WITH PHASES

CAUTION

Let's step back and review our five change strategies: awareness, understanding, participation, measurement, and leverage. It was easy to see how awareness preceded understanding. Until employees were aware of something, they could not fully understand it. It would thus seem that participation should come next, and that would be correct.

The word *phase* implies a one-directional, sequential flow of activities, but a change initiative isn't like that. One group of people may already understand something and be participating in it, while another group is just becoming aware of the same thing. Because your work in building awareness, understanding, and participation will be ongoing, I've titled them *"strategies," and not phases.* Think of each strategy as a lever—which you pull individually or in combination to achieve results.

Building Active Participation

It is simple to *say* the word *participation*. But how do you actually help people to participate? When do you expand your team? How do you get the participation you want? As a manager, you may have a long list of questions about how participation can work with the various challenges of a change operation.

To foster participation, as we discussed in Chapter 7, let's assume you have already helped employees understand what the change means:

THE MONSTERS UNDER THE BED

With change comes fear. A lot of fear, however, is unfounded. Think of a child who imagines monsters under the bed. No amount of dialogue will dissolve the fear. Until you are willing to take the child's hand and venture with him under the bed to see firsthand that there are no monsters, you haven't yet convinced him to let go of his fear. Similarly, people experiencing change also need their hands held. But it's not enough *just* to hold their hands. If you want full engagement, take them under the bed to see that it's not scary at all. Only then will you create participation.

- At an enterprise level
- At a work team level
- At an individual level

You are now ready to engage participation in this change by encouraging fellow employees to:

- Self-assess how they can participate
- Actively assist in the redesign of business processes
- Carry forth messages in a trustworthy way
- Help their peers and subordinates commit to change

AN ENGAGING LEADER

FOR EXAMPLE

Recently, I was working with a board of directors introducing an initiative that constituted a distinct change in direction—and was guaranteed to ruffle feathers. The change leader was very public about how people would be selected as members of the change team. Over and over, in forum after forum, the leader stated his criteria. Initially, he asked for input on areas still being developed. Eventually, he stopped asking for input, but kept stating the decided-upon criteria.

A week before the rollout, a board member suggested adding new and very different selection criteria. The leader handled it well. Rather than attack the merits of the person's suggestion, he turned the conversation toward the process: "Folks, we have discussed the criteria on several occasions. Although I always value input, we need to move forward with what we have already agreed on. This new idea can be incorporated at a later time." The leader was essentially saying, "Because I asked for your input on selection criteria long ago, I am not going to slow down the process because you want to provide it now." There would be no derailing and no attacks on the board member's suggestion. People's participation would be welcome, but it would be according to a schedule.

Let's start by thinking through some of the typical steps in a change program, and how you can build participation throughout the organization. Table 8-1 lists typical *steps* taken in the change process, *who might be involved*, and *how* these people can be engaged to participate in the change initiative.

Project Step	Who Might Be Involved	How They Might Participate
Establishing a Vision and Resources for the Project	A project sponsor The sponsor's management The sponsor's peers	Provide guidance/set urgency Provide support Allocate resources Identify criteria for success
Designing a New Organizational Structure	Human resources Information technology	Identify legal and policy risks Redesign processes and reports to support the new design
Developing a Business Continuity Plan	Customers Suppliers	Develop goodwill to support you when there are transition issues
Building a Risk Plan	Managers	Assess impacts on their own organizations Stand up in front of management and take accountability for managing risks and results in their area
Training Workforce	Trainers	Become trained to be a trainer Provide peer-to-peer support

Table 8-1. Steps, involvement, and participation during the change process

In Chapter 11, I discuss how roles and responsibilities can be clarified through a formal governance process. For now, know there is a role for many people to participate in your change program. Once a sponsor asks for a change to be initiated, those people come into play.

> **KEY TERM** **Sponsor** The change initiative you are tasked with supporting will have a sponsor. This person is the single point of account-ability for the initiative's success and typically has business-oriented definitions of success. Your sponsor will know that reaching those definitions of success will depend on getting the organization to support the initiative. He or she will see you as the expert on getting the organization where it needs to go.
>
> For both of you to be successful, you will need a strong relationship. You and the sponsor will want to establish ground rules in your relationship that include:
>
> - Honesty
> - Candidness
> - Trust
>
> The reality is, the sponsor may be two levels above you on the organization chart, but you must be able to speak openly to be valuable. You may be entering new ground, but with it comes the opportunity to learn about how your leadership thinks and operates.

Who Should Participate in the Change Process— Four Key Roles

Four roles are critical to your participation strategy and the project's success. The four key roles in a typical change project are:

1. **Leaders and managers.** Every company needs solid leadership and management, as does every change initiative. People in this role should be solid communicators capable of providing directives and influencing buy-in.

2. **Subject matter experts.** SMEs are the core of your project team. They bring expertise from many areas. They are your strength and backbone during the course of the project.

3. **Trainers.** As we discussed in Chapter 7, many change projects requires training. The need for training is obvious on a change initiative such as implementing a new system, where your employees need to learn new software. The need for employee education also exists, however, in non-technology-related changes where the workforce needs to learn how to *act differently* during and after the change initiative.

4. **Super users.** In a technology project, users always require support after go-live. Super users provide peer-to-peer support and train new

employees in how to perform their jobs. They provide the organizational glue in the change project—ensuring that it lasts over the long haul—because they continue to train and educate employees as they come and go. They are frequently overlooked at the start of any initiative.

THE FIFTH ROLE: YOU **SMART**

You are the person who supports the project sponsor as he or she leads people through the change process. You will **MANAGING** be a tireless advocate for the sponsor's vision. You will also be a tireless advocate for the needs of the people who need to change. (Of course, the conversations about the organization's needs occur behind closed doors. You and the sponsor must always be aligned.)

See Table 8-2 for an illustration of where these critical roles fit into each stage of the change, as we introduced in Figure 7-1.

Prepare	Design	Build	Test	Train	Support
Leadership				Leadership	
	SMEs	SMEs	SMEs	SMEs	SMEs
			Trainers	Trainers	Trainers
			Super Users	Super Users	Super Users

Table 8-2. Critical activity periods for each role

Know When to Call Your People In, and When to Hold Off

Be deliberate when involving people and ensure that the right people are involved at the right times. For example, *doers* may get frustrated when put in a planning or brainstorming role; similarly, *brainstormers* may not have the right level of detailed experience to take part in the implementation phase. The key lies in determining when to include them. Get your brainstorming idea people involved early, but plan to pull them out of the way once the project rolls into implementation. Implementation is not the time to make changes on the fly! Similarly, when it is time to figure out how to make something really work, involve the experts at getting things done. They will prevent many issues from arising later.

You also need to be sensitive to personality traits. Let's create a hypothetical situation. A sponsor or leader decides to take a group on a car trip to another city. Now is not the time to include the group grump. He will throw up obstacles: "Bad idea." "Wrong city." "Car trips are dangerous." The list will be long, and the group grump has the ability to spoil the trip. My advice: Don't include him!

Similarly, don't wait until the end to include him. You will hear all the original complaints, but now you will also hear about bad seats, bad scenery, poor uses of time, and how the trip costs too much.

Instead, involve him in the middle: after the basics of the trip have been decided, but before all the details are set. Introducing him at this point gives him the opportunity to complain about it being a bad idea, a bad city, and a dangerous venture. He can also complain about the way the trip will be conducted. Your task is to turn his diffused negative energy into focused positive energy. For example, he may have complaints about the budget and food. You can engage his participation by saying: "That is right, Jim. Having the right food supplies and getting it done within budget will be important and are issues for us. Could I ask you to be in charge of the food?"

Engaging the grump in determining how your program goes forward allows your concept to get off the ground, gives you another set of hands to get the work done, ensures you understand his concerns, and minimizes the risk of sabotage.

Similarly, involve your employees in the change initiative at the key times—when you can communicate your vision and goals, foster participation and buy-in, and avoid opening up your efforts to being undermined. Then, listen for ways to involve employees in finding even better solutions to your tactical issues.

MOVING FROM THEORY TO PRACTICE

TOOLS Make a simple table with the following columns: Person, Strengths, Weaknesses, Skills, Experiences, Ways They Can Help Your Project. List the people who could be impacted by the project or who might be able to help you. Work on this list at your local coffee shop where you have the opportunity to really think about each person. You will be surprised at how many people you know who can participate in positive ways on your project.

How the Four Key Roles Participate

People in the four key roles have different responsibilities in a change intiative.

Role #1: Leaders

My rule of thumb on whether something is a big change is if two levels above the sponsor are aware of the initiative. That would include if it is a company-wide initiative. For example, are investors, customers, or suppliers aware?

If I use my rule of thumb, a leader would include anybody in the sponsor's management, as well as his or her organizational peers. If this is a company-wide initiative, leaders would include the C-suite (CEO, COO, CFO, CIO, etc.), vice presidents, and directors who show strong leadership skills.

Leaders should be able to discuss the big picture of the change and the details that are appropriate for their area of responsibility. They should model the behaviors they want employees to demonstrate and proactively direct others toward achieving goals. In an ideal world, they each send the same positive message about the change. We discuss in later chapters how you get your leaders to work like a synchronized swimming team.

Role #2: Subject Matter Experts (SMEs)

An SME holds multiple responsibilities. He or she typically:

- Fully understands how things operated in the past and current state and can envision how the future state must function to be considered a success.
- Designs business processes and organizations to meet business objectives. Provides ongoing feedback on the change feasibility study, project scope, and overall design decisions.
- In technical systems change projects, works with the technical team on pertinent information technology support structure changes; for culture change projects, works with leadership or the HR department to interpret how business changes may positively or negatively impact the business culture.
- Gains the support of the steering committee for changes to current

ways of working and serves as an expert to the steering committee. Identifies potential options to the steering committee regarding ways to organize the company's structure.

■ Tests the capability of the new processes, technology, and organizational structures to deliver the benefits predicted in the original design.

■ Is responsible for ensuring that end user training materials and job aids accurately reflect the new ways of working.

■ Communicates regularly with stakeholders.

WHAT MAKES A GOOD SME?   SMART

A good SME has a combination of the following:

■ Experience in a past change initiative
■ Ability to hold respect of peers
■ Effective communication skills

MANAGING

■ Ability to project a can-do optimism throughout the project while spreading that optimism to others
■ Ability to optimize the organization as a whole, even if it means a burden of work may shift onto himself or herself
■ Ability to operate in a confidential manner

Extending your project team. Your success will come when the workforce is clear about their roles and tasks. An organization that operates purely on "tribal knowledge" will soon revert to an unproductive state. The challenge is that documenting how a company is supposed to work can be daunting. The team SMEs may not have enough time to get the new design documented.

At this point, you should consider enlarging your project team and incorporating new members to document how the organization will work in the future. Your leadership might question why you are involved in designing the size of the project team, but you really are coming at things from a change management perspective. You are helping the organization move through change by having more people participate in creating the future, reducing the learning curve when you go through the actual change, and reducing the apprehension of the change throughout the organization. If you tell your leadership that participation is one of your strategies, they will understand when you start asking for people to participate.

AN SME BY OTHER NAMES

SMART MANAGING

SMEs can also be called *champions, stewards,* or *owners.* The distinctions are subtle and often interchangeable.

Champions: SME implies a competent expert. Champion implies an advocate—like what you get when you cross an SME with a cheerleader.

Owners: The best SMEs have the ability to look outside their areas of responsibility and think about the greater good—to act as owners. They are highly accountable individuals.

Process Stewards: The best SMEs practice a process called stewardship, which we detail in Chapter 12. A steward takes care of things that aren't theirs because they know it is the right thing to do.

I suggest you influence what your SMEs are called, as names create culture. For example, if you have a culture of low accountability, naming someone an *owner* forces him or her to step up to accountability. Alternatively, if you have a hierarchical and structured organization, naming somebody who will work across functions as an *owner* is likely to threaten and upset those who will not welcome an intrusion into their areas of responsibility.

The work the SMEs do will be instrumental for three reasons, as it will:

1. **Capture knowledge.** Information in this document will be used as a foundation for education and training materials, communications, work design, and change management activities. In other words, creating the blueprint on the front end saves time and resources during the training and implementation phases.

2. **Provide detail.** This document's information should include a level of detail that shows how work will actually be executed in business units.

3. **Create alignment on how the change will be implemented.** In conjunction with business unit line management, the process blueprint will identify how individual business units will implement and execute particular business processes in the change-enabled environment. The carpenter adage applies here: "Measure twice, cut once." Likewise, your blueprint allows each business unit to "measure" the impacts on its own unit, and it allows for dialogues that may cut off unexpected problems before anything gets "cut."

The documentation might include:

- Process flow or diagram
- Documentation of what is not on the flow (reports, forms, policies, procedures, etc.)
- Audit and control considerations
- Roles and responsibilities

Role #3: Trainers

Trainers should be educators instead of sages or entertainers. Educators are passionate about seeing others learn, master information, and apply what they learn successfully; sages and entertainers like the limelight and the sound of their own voices. Participants might enjoy sages and entertainers, but you should focus instead on finding trainers who value

---

SMART

MANAGING

ENGAGE MILLENIALS

According to a recent study, 66 percent of CEOs have said that finding and keeping talent is a challenge. In fact, three-quarters of companies have had to postpone initiatives because they couldn't find the talent they needed. Even in a struggling economy when jobless rates soar—and perhaps especially in a down economy—the right people are critical to your company's success. You need them more than ever to deliver their talent and participate in your change efforts.

Millenials make up a large portion of the hiring pool. According to Pew Research, Millennials account for 37 percent of the workforce (www.cap strat.com/ elements/downloads/files/millennials-work.pdf)! We've all heard the complaints from managers trying to lead Millennials but having no idea how to engage them. Maybe you've heard some of these common complaints or comments about this generation of workers:

- They've been told their entire lives how wonderful they are, and instead of being smart or experienced, they're just incredibly arrogant!
- They come to work to socialize and play. They can't live without being attached to a smartphone in one hand and a tablet in the next!
- Even though they love technology, they have a need for too much *face time* and one-on-one coaching and interaction.
- I just don't understand them.

You can complain about them or stereotype them if you want, but I can tell you from my experience that millennials want to participate. If you take the approach in a change project of not incorporating their input, you are doing long-term strategic damage to your company—because you will be pushing away talent that is key to your future success.

learning as the highest objective. Trainers should be well versed in adult learning theory, know the content they deliver, and package it effectively. And they should have the credibility and presentation skills that facilitate learning. For more on training, refer to Chapter 7.

WHEN ROLES OVERLAP

In large organizations with a vast pool of employees who represent specific skill sets, you can likely assign a specific change role to each person. In small organizations, however, sometimes the same person will need to fill more than one role. Be creative in your assignments, and assign roles based on each person's skills.

Role #4 Super Users

If you implemented a new program today, you first rallied the troops and prepared them to do something new—training them until they became competent. Once they became competent, productivity accelerated and your company became competitive in the marketplace. This was great—but what will happen next?

Employees will quit and be replaced. New employees will come on board and receive less training—leading

Erosion The gradual decline in productivity that occurs over time if a change is not made sustainable.   **KEY TERM**

to lower productivity. As a result, subsequent changes may be poorly implemented. Or, a new group may not know why a change was made, and thus might plan a change that would take the company back—wasting time and potentially repeating mistakes.

This decline in productivity over time is known as *erosion* (see Figure 8-1).

Specific causes of erosion include:

- Insufficient post-go-live refresher training
- Lack of ownership for business process competency post-go-live
- Little monitoring of required competencies
- Insufficient appreciation (rewards, compensation) of competencies
- No succession planning
- Overdependence on third-party support that will eventually go away

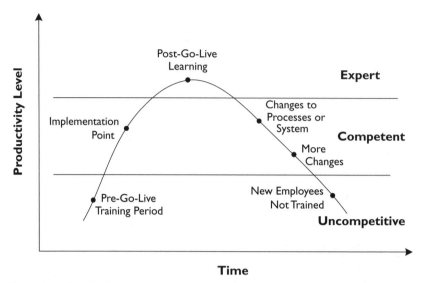

Figure 8-1. Erosion

Assigning super users prevents erosion. The super user ensures that the initial change is lasting, and all subsequent changes are forward moving—because he or she keeps the organization up-to-date and aware of the key aspects surrounding the change. The super user ensures that onboarding, training, and succession planning occur efficiently.

A well-structured, well-organized, effective super-user community is crucial for sustainability. Super users deliver peer-to-peer support in a technology change. Super users hold the most knowledge about the new business processes. They serve as the key resources over time as new employees come on board, old employees leave, or additional changes occur. Details of your project may change—in terms of who is involved, the geographical boundaries, the organizational dynamics, the complexity, etc.—but your super users remain to offer peer-to-peer

> **TRICKS OF THE TRADE**
>
> **ASSIGNING SUPER USERS**
>
> Be creative in who you assign this role. Often, I've found the best super users among the administrative assistants of senior staff—such as the vice presidents. Admins at the senior or C-suite level come into proximity with key information and need to know how to work the new systems to support their bosses and other employees. A panel of C-suite or VP admins can create a powerful super-user team.

organizational support. The super users become your SMEs after your change is in place.

In a nontechnology change, you may not have a super user in the traditional sense. Identifying the person who is the most "in the know" about the topic at hand, however, still holds value in ensuring your change sticks.

A company that fails to assign a super user is a clear example of a business that hasn't paid enough attention to the organizational structures needed to make the change stay in place. Managing your processes, supporting your users, and continuously improving your performance must be seen as strategic imperatives. You can use your own term if you like, but you must have people filling the role of super users. This implementation remains key to protecting your investment and creating sustainability in your change effort.

Many of Us Already Know How to Build a Change Plan

Let's say you need to prepare your child for his first day of kindergarten. As the parent, you make an effort to understand his level of enthusiasm—or fear—about starting this new phase of his life. You help him mark off the days on the calendar as you count down to the beginning of school. You take him on a tour of the building, introduce him to the teacher, and even drive him along the bus route. You bring him with you to the store to buy school supplies and a backpack, and help him choose the outfit he will wear to class. You let him decide what special treats he wants in his lunch for the big day. You help the child understand his role as a kindergartener, and you conduct some dry run trips to the school and bus stop to create participation.

When the big day arrives, you're there to make him his favorite breakfast, accompany him to the bus stop, and wave as he and other children start their adventures. And that evening, you eagerly listen to his account of what his first day of school was like—and help him get ready for the next.

Using the three strategies, you built a change plan for your kindergartener. You took your child though a series of logical steps to help him get ready—in every respect—for the beginning of his school career. Your prevailing concern throughout the entire process was to help him adjust and adapt easily and quickly. In other words, you helped to create, led, and manage the change in his life. You made your child aware of kindergarten. You built understanding through dialogue. And you helped him participate. His head, heart, and hands became involved.

One of the most important objectives of your change initiative is to engage team members to help them feel like owners in the change—so that they will say, as in the quote that started this chapter, "We did it ourselves." Like the kindergartener who eventually feels confident enough with his role in the school that he can say, "I did it myself," employees who feel like owners will be more apt to help you make the change not only sustainable, but effective.

In the next chapters, I show how to supercharge these concepts and make your work easier.

Manager's Checklist for Chapter 8

☑ Participation makes a change effort more effective because it allows you as a manager to get out of the way and engage your team of experts to own the roles most suitable to them.

☑ Increasing participation is hard at first, but it makes your job easier in the long run.

☑ Assign people to the key roles, including champions, change agents, leaders, SMEs, trainers, and super users.

☑ Super users offer key peer-to-peer organizational support for and knowledge of the new system, making your change effort sustainable even through additional change or turnover. Super users are particularly key as third-party support wanes. They forestall knowledge and productivity erosion.

☑ Know when to integrate feedback from others into the change plan, and when to simply communicate what will happen.

Using Leverage to Ease the Effort

Give me a lever long enough and a fulcrum on which to place it, and I shall move the world.

—Archimedes

Let me make a prediction. If you follow the recommendations regarding awareness, understanding, and participation, you will be busy. Depending on the project you work on, you may be answering questions at a frenetic pace like a child playing a game of whack-a-mole. Or you might find yourself perpetually squelching the rumor of the day, playing the role of the fictional Dutch boy who stuck his finger in the dike to stop the leak. It's not uncommon for change management practitioners to feel like they are whack-a-mole-ing and plugging a dike simultaneously!

Don't let my next comment discourage you, but you can't possibly fill the role of change manager alone. Now let me amend that slightly: you *can* be successful if you execute a strategy that multiplies your efforts. I call this strategy *leverage*.

You want to be able to press down in one place and create exponential energy in another place. That is what the quote at the top of this chapter means. Archimedes was explaining the concept of a seesaw. If you make the seesaw long enough, you can press down with one finger and lift the weight of a person. Carried to its natural extension, a lever long enough can lift the world. This chapter is going to show you how to magnify your efforts with the leverage created by force multipliers.

Let's go back to Chapter 2 where I shared a chart (Figure 2-2) illustrating the tendency to underresource change initiatives. Typical change initiatives don't have enough time, money, or people assigned to them. What does it take to move the world or, in change management, to implement a successful change initiative? Your "fulcrum" in a change initiative is the point around which you will pivot the organization. The "lever long enough" is the group of resources (like time, budget, and staff) you will use to move the organization.

SMART MANAGING

LEVERAGE IS LIKE BOWLING

If the concept of leverage brings back bad memories of high school physics classes, think of another example: bowling. If you hit the #1 pin just right, you can knock down all 10 pins. Miss the head pin, and you won't get them all. You might even have to attack the dreaded 7–10 split!

The important thing to understand about leverage is that there are actions you can take to lengthen your lever. We discuss how to stretch and create resources where none are provided.

How do you lengthen and use the lever to provide your change program with extra force to move an organization that doesn't want to move? You do so through leverage. The concepts of leverage I cover in this chapter are:

- When to build your leverage program
- Leadership alignment
- Stakeholder management
- Change agent networks
- Create once; use many times

When to Build Your Leverage Program

Before going into detail, I want to make one point clear: Your success depends on your planning a leverage strategy prior to when you actually need it. You need leverage, and the only way to create that leverage is by having a plan that ensures your lever is in place well before you need it.

In some respects, being a change manager is like being a political campaign manager. Your job is to convince people to take action on behalf of the politician (the candidate corresponds to your sponsor). I'd be willing to bet that your first action as campaign manager would be to shape and understand the politician's key messages. Your second action would be to build your team. You would then seek financial backing, additional campaign staff, and lots of volunteers. If you ever ran for eighth grade class president, you probably held a party around the activity of getting your friends to make campaign signs. The concepts in change management are the same. Ask yourself: Who are your volunteers? And how do you get them engaged and ready during the first days of the project so they are there to call on when needed? The point is: Build that core support long before you need it. When you need it, you won't have the time to build it.

Leadership Alignment

Before we dig into the concept of "leadership alignment," let's make sure we as reader and author are aligned on some assumptions about a change initiative. We talk more about project governance in Chapter 11, but the typical project I encounter is managed as follows:

- **Sponsor.** The sponsor is the single point of accountability for the project. Even if a day-to-day project manager exists, the sponsor is intimately involved in all aspects of the project.
- **Executive sponsor.** The sponsor will have a supervisor who is frequently called the executive sponsor.
- **The steering committee.** The steering committee is frequently made up of the sponsor's peers, with potential representation from individuals one level up in the organization. The members can be hands-on and active, like a board of directors, or more passive, like an advisory board.
- **Stakeholders.** Stakeholders have direct or indirect "skin in the game" in the form of having something to gain or lose by the change's success—making them potential powerful advocates or adversaries for a change initiative and its outcome. Stakeholders may be employees, customers, or even vendors.

 **THE OUT-OF-STEP LEADER**

If leaders don't speak as one in public, work with the out-of-step leader directly to create stronger alignment. If you aren't successful in fostering alignment, you have a responsibility to bring the issue to the attention of the sponsor to avoid undermining the project.

These groups of people will have different points of view when they meet, but they need to agree when they are in front of the workforce. Getting them aligned at the start is critical.

To get your leaders, meaning sponsor, steering committee, and senior-level stake-

MANAGEMENT HEADACHES

A human resources professional recently asked me how he could help his company become better at managing change.

I felt a bit like the doctor answering the question, "I have a bad headache; what's wrong with me?"

Without more information, the answer would have been simple: "Take two aspirin, and call me in the morning," both for the change challenge as well as the headache.

Resisting the urge to encourage him to call my office, I gave my diagnosis-free prescription: "Improve senior management leadership capabilities." When organizations create senior leaders with deep skills and experience in managing change, the results of the current change initiatives improve. The leaders' strengths also provide leverage for future initiatives.

holders, aligned, you need to have a conversation with them to understand their perspectives. I suggest discussing the following topics with each of them individually at the beginning of the project. Ask:

1. Please tell me about the largest change initiatives you've gone through in the last five to seven years.
2. What went well with those initiatives, and what did not go well?
3. How likely are we to go through large-scale change in the next three years?
4. How likely are we to repeat the positives and negatives of your previous experiences?
5. How well prepared are our senior and middle managers to lead future changes?
6. What should we do now to best prepare for the future?

After having these individual conversations, bring them together as a group to discuss their answers. In preparation for that meeting, I suggest you do the following homework:

1. Cluster the *common themes* you learned from your individual senior leadership interviews. Make a list of items, not who said what. In addition to what you learned from the themes that surfaced, you will gain strong insight into how the leadership group thinks and views the organization's change readiness.

2. Identify the *conflicting themes* you gleaned from your senior leadership interviews. List any conflicting information you heard, but once again, do not note who said what. You want to be seen as an objective, collaborative expert, and not someone who stirs the pot on irrelevant issues. Like the list of common themes, the conflicting reports you hear can help you gain insight on individual leaders' hot buttons or areas of concerns. Those clues can help you guide and structure your resources later to proactively address potential concerns.

3. Research *best practices* and experiences of other organizations. This will allow you to build on your cultural and organizational strengths while minimizing your risks and potential liabilities.

4. Develop a list of *concrete recommendations* to share at the meeting. Remember, the senior leaders are busy, and they expect you—as the change expert—to have done your own due diligence and spent time preparing the thoughtful, relevant information they need to know. By respecting leaders' time while providing expert advice, you build a reputation with them that you can leverage in the future. At the meeting, summarize what you found in your homework and research, such as:

   - Here are the *common themes* I heard from my time with you.
   - Here are a few nuances I heard from my time with you that indicate there might be some room for *continuous improvement* around future initiatives.
   - Here are the *best practices* I found compared to the common themes I heard from you.
   - Here are my *recommendations* for addressing opportunities and minimizing risks around future change initiatives.

SMART MANAGING

LEADERS AS THE LEVER
As you engage with leaders, you also gain the ability to draw on them later in the project (as your lever), and you can better anticipate what they will say (your fulcrum).

TRICKS OF THE TRADE

LEADERS UNITE
You want leaders to be properly aligned and to agree on objectives, principles, ways of working, and key messages at the outset. Ensuring that leaders are aligned to the change initiative will set the stage for creating an aligned workforce. When employees work as a united front, the change process can remain positive. If they don't work together, employees will not see the program as a priority.

As you might imagine, your list of recommendations could cover a wide range of options, but people-related opportunities are likely to dominate. The best part of this approach is that the go-forward plan will be crafted largely based on the specific feedback from the senior leaders.

If leaders aren't on board with the change—or aren't visible throughout the process, people are not going to see the change as important. People will reason that the change might be a cause for apprehension if they don't witness their leaders personally endorsing and engaging in the change.

C.R.E.A.T.E. a Thriving Change Environment

Having engaged and engaging leaders is critical to preparation for the change, and is imperative in training, at go-live, and immediately following the onset of the change. When the masses are learning how to operate in a new environment, tensions will be high. During times of change and tension, leaders need to remember that they are responsible to C.R.E.A.T.E. the environment where change thrives:

Compliment. We've all had days when everything that could go wrong has gone wrong, and no matter what good we strived to accomplish, the only feedback we heard sounded like criticisms and "you-should-haves." Assume there will be tough times in your change initiative when what you and others will need most is a sincere compliment. A compliment spelling out what people have done well lightens the load of the hard work it took to achieve that stellar result. *Leaders, create additional* *change-ready leaders by handing out compliments, not critiques.*

Reassure. According to most definitions, reassure means to *restore to confidence.* This implies that leaders have to be on the lookout for deflated confidence in need of a recharge. How can a leader reassure? There's magic in the phrase "It's going to be okay" when said by someone people trust and respect. Parents say this to their children to soothe them during thunderstorms, and strong leaders utter similar phrases to teams who need a little boost to know that they are heading in the right direction, doing the right things—and will be generating outstanding results.

Encourage. Encouragement goes beyond reassurance. Instead of merely restoring employee confidence that may have waned, to encourage means to *inspire with courage.* Leaders may or may not be subject matter experts, but all strong, positive leaders know how to inspire others, which literally means to *breathe life* into others.

> **Inspiro** This Latin word means:
>
> 1. blow on/into
> 2. breathe into
> 3. excite, inflame
> 4. inspire
> 5. instill, implant
>
> **KEY TERM**
>
> In your management, as you inspire others, think of it as giving them breath and "flame" to proceed.

Ask. Sometimes people with high titles in an organization get more accustomed to *telling* instead of *asking.* Certainly, your boss has the right to tell you what he or she wants you to do. But that's not what powerful leaders do. Engaging leaders are careful to *ask*, not *tell.* The act of asking, "Would you be willing to . . . " or, "There's something I'd like you to do," demonstrates a level of respect that is almost always reciprocated with outstanding employee results. So, what I'm asking you is: "Would you replace what you *tell* your employees to do with *asking* them to help?"

Thank. Sometimes, the smallest phases are the most powerful. After an argument, what most people want to hear is "I'm sorry." When saying good-bye to a loved one, what most people want to hear is, "I love you." And working tirelessly to reach a project goal, deadline, or new milestone, what most people want to hear is "Thank you." It's that simple. In English grammar, it's acceptable at times to use something called "the implied you." For example, it's acceptable to say or write, "Come in here, please," instead of "You come in here, please," because *you* is implied. I say this to reinforce a point: there is no rule called "the implied thank you." Say it. Say it often, say it sincerely, and say it broadly to those you lead. Hearing a thank-you makes employees want to give you a repeat performance of what earned the first thank you.

Embody. I could have chosen the word *model,* but the word *embody* is more powerful (and if I used the model, it would spell C.R.E.A.T.M., which is not a word!). To embody is *to personify and exemplify in a concrete way.* In other words, a leader who *embodies* engaging change leadership isn't merely putting on a white hat and using a checklist that prompts him to act a certain way. No, an engaging leader *is* the type of person who wants every employee to copy him or her. Leadership is not a role; it's a state of being.

SMART MANAGING

CREATING BUY-IN BY NAME-DROPPING

To accelerate corporate change initiatives using leverage, you need a secret weapon: Find the highest-level executive you can to buy into and support the vision. Getting a top leader to endorse the vision for the change initiative will create more ready, eager followers on the front end. When you say things like "When I was speaking to our CEO, she fully agreed with the direction we are heading," you're more likely to catch the attention of employees than if you say, "Well, I mentioned this idea to a friend, and he rather liked it."

To better understand the leverage this tactic can create, let's look at how this philosophy is used in sales. Several prominent training programs ask salespeople to start their process by calling one level above their key contacts. Then, the salespeople call their key contacts and state, "Your boss, John, said I should talk to you about this . . ."

Keeping Alignment Means Managing Your Stakeholders

So you followed the advice above and your leadership is all aligned and moving forward, right? How long do you think this alignment and forward movement will last on its own? My guess is about two weeks. Politics, turnover, changing priorities, and fear of change will ensure that all the key people who have a stake in the success of your initiative eventually will head off in their own directions. Their movement won't be like a bowling ball knocking down pins; it will be like a cue ball that sends all the billiard balls in random directions. Your job is to ensure that everybody is working toward the same goals.

LAZY LEADERS

Lazy leaders say to their change managers, "You're the change manager. You go communicate." People watch what their leaders say and don't say. When leaders don't talk—but instead outsource communications to the change guy—it sends a powerful yet destructive message to the masses: *What this guy is saying isn't important.*

Let's say, for example, that a manager in your HR department sends out a memo about changes to your group's dental plan. The fact that a manager is sending out that message might lead some employees to assume that it is relevant only to those at the manager level and below. On the other hand, if your CEO hands out a memo to all employees at the corporate cafeteria about changes in your group's dental plan, employees get the message that *this is important!* Why? *If it's important enough to get the CEO out on the cafeteria floor,* they think, *it certainly must be important to me!* Similarly, if the change manager is the only one talking, the change project is doomed. You need to get everyone talking—especially leadership.

Stakeholder management consists of the following steps:

- **Identify.** You need to know who each person is and his or her position in the organization.
- **Analyze.** You need to know:
  - The relative importance of each stakeholder to the success of your project, as well as how each stakeholder might derail progress toward the goals your sponsor has laid out.
  - Each stakeholder's goals and how they align to your project's goals.
  - How each stakeholder will be impacted by the project and their resulting actions and attitudes.
- **Engage.** Be sure to:
  - Communicate what's important to them, and keep them fully apprised of what's important to your sponsor.
  - Communicate the relevant thoughts of key stakeholders to the sponsor.
  - Place each of the stakeholders on a regular contact schedule—particularly those on the top half of the chart (see sidebar Stakeholder Influence Map on page 133).

REVERSE LEVERAGE

CAUTION

Change sponsors—and by extension the people who are help-ing the change sponsors lead the change initiatives—have a pre-cious asset: their credibility. "Playing it straight" is absolutely crucial.

Should you as a change manager ever take a shortcut past the full truth, you will get caught. When you get caught, everybody will find out. When they find out, they will second-guess everything you say. If you have to go into your change initiative with reduced credibility, you will find that leading that change will become all the harder. Nobody likes to follow somebody who doesn't tell the truth. This creates the opposite of leverage—your lack of credibility actually diminishes your position.

MAKE A LIST

Imagine the sponsor is the president of the United States. You are the secretary of state. Your job is to manage U.S. relations with all the other countries in the world. You might pay more attention to Canada than Iceland and more attention to China than Australia—depending on what is going on in those countries and how they rank as stakeholders. Think about who are all the people you're responsible for keeping track of and how you should prioritize them.

- Know when your ability to appropriately manage a stakeholder is at risk. If an important stakeholder isn't responding to you as needed, you need to call in help from the sponsor.

Change Agents

In any change project, you're going to have lots of stakeholders to con-tact. This work is on top of all the other work that has been assigned to you. How do you get it done?

The answer lies in the force multiplier of change agents.

The best people to help employees throughout the change process are their direct supervisors. But how do you reach all the direct supervi-sors? Think back to the bowling ball. To knock down all the pins in the back row, you first need to get the pins in the front. Thanks to your lead-ership alignment plan, you have the first three pins covered. You have awareness, understanding, and participation cascading from the sponsor to the VPs, who then touch the directors, who touch the managers, and so

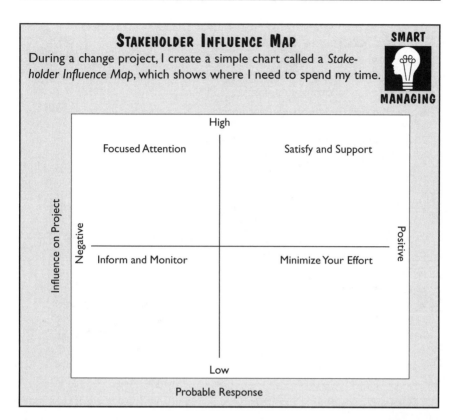

STAKEHOLDER INFLUENCE MAP

SMART

MANAGING

During a change project, I create a simple chart called a *Stakeholder Influence Map*, which shows where I need to spend my time.

SMART NEGOTIATING

TRICKS OF THE TRADE

I went to a negotiating class, and the most important thing I learned was to meet every request with a return request. By doing so, you force the person you are negotiating with to respect you. In my own home, I would never expect dinner to be made for me without being asked to clean up afterward. Similarly, in stakeholder management, the stakeholder's request for you to "tell the sponsor that he needs to do x, y, and z" should be met with something like "I will certainly do so, but could I ask you to make sure you cover these three points with your direct reports next week?" This type of response gives you the opportunity to follow up at your next meeting and ask if this has been done. You may gulp hard the first time you do this with someone much higher in the organization, but it does get easier over time.

on. The formal network works through cascading—as people communicate to their direct reports.

STAKEHOLDER MANAGEMENT SPREADSHEET

Create a spreadsheet to track all your stakeholders. Regularly review this stakeholder management spreadsheet with your sponsor. Include the following columns:

TOOLS

- Stakeholder Group Name (this enables you to sort the list by groups)
- Stakeholder Name
- Stakeholder Title
- Stakeholder Role in the Organization
- Stakeholder Potential Impact on Project (simple 1 to 5 ranking)
- What Is in It for Them (a notes field to describe how to best position the project with the stakeholder)
- Project Impact on Stakeholder (high, medium, or low positive, and high, medium, or low negative)
- Required Level of Support (simple 1 to 5 ranking)
- Current Level of Support (simple 1 to 5 ranking)
- Stakeholder Perspectives (a notes field to keep track of the stakeholder's point of view)
- Actions and Recommendations (a notes field to keep track of what should be done next)
- Date of Next Appointment

But you must realize that this formal cascading doesn't work perfectly. As a change manager, you must recognize that you won't be able to reach all leaders this way. VPs are busy—talking to customers, etc.—so you need a backstop. That backstop consists of the second component: change agents.

When organized into an informal network, your change agent network is your Plan B—advocating on behalf of the change even when you or your leaders can't. A change agent may help catalyze the change, improve the process, secure top-notch resources, and engage others in pivotal roles through your change initiative.

Specifically, a change agent may be responsible for:

- Overcoming shortcomings in cascading information through the business.
- Minimizing business disruptions by providing, on a face-to-face basis, team managers and associates with much of the information

they need to understand the changes happening in the business.

- Promoting team and individual understanding of the value of your change and its requirements for work processes, practices, and behaviors.

- Routinely gathering feedback from peer leaders and associates to address questions, concerns, and potential roadblocks in a timely manner. In other words, change agents can give you "the word on the street."

> **WHY YOU NEED CHANGE AGENTS** — **SMART MANAGING**
>
>
>
> Even if your leadership is aligned, change agents don't pitch in to help you every day. They have other things that take up their time. The same can be said of those at the levels below management. For example, if on a given day 80 percent of your VPs communicate about your change to 80 percent of those at the director level, who in turn communicate it to 80 percent of those at the manager level, only 51.2 percent of managers will receive this message (80 percent times 80 percent times 80 percent). If you extend this down one more level, you only have 40 percent of people receiving the message—and 40 percent is not adequate to bring about change.

- Encouraging teams and individuals to accept and adopt their new responsibilities and to self-assess how they can make a meaningful contribution to your organization's success.

- Recognizing team- and individual-specific wins in connection with your preparation, training, and go-live. Champion your company by acting as a visible and credible role model.

Commanding the respect of peer leaders as well as associates, the change agent must project a passion for your effort—a conviction that it will meet its goals and objectives —and confidence in others to work together to reach milestones in accord with the proposed timeline for execution. Ideally, change agent candidates must have the respect of

> **CHANGE AGENT COMMUNICATIONS** — **TRICKS OF THE TRADE**
>
> Regular communications with your change agents will ensure ongoing leverage. I suggest conducting a weekly conference call. Make sure the call is dialogue oriented. Dispense a list of talking points or takeaways from the call to accommodate different learning styles, and ensure the main points are consistently understood and represented.

WHAT MAKES A GOOD CHANGE AGENT?

SMART

The best change agents are:

1. Respected by their peers
2. Proactive communicators
3. Competent—particularly in your ways of working and in the company culture

MANAGING

4. Able to navigate through ambiguous, unstable, and/or challenging circumstances
5. Talented in negotiation, problem resolution, and consensus development
6. Sensitive, tactful, and able to influence and persuade without coercing
7. In possession of a sense of humor, positive disposition, and can-do attitude
8. Willing to follow directions while advocating for the right direction
9. Eager to act

Remember the description of subject matter experts? SMEs need to be experts in your business, with a bit of people skills. Change agents need to be highly skilled with people, with a more modest level of business competency.

Ensuring that change agents are inspired to ignite passion for your change requires that you provide them with adequate information about the change. The best way to do this is through regular communications with all change agents.

peer leaders and associates alike for their achievements to result in rapid decision making, stewardship of company resources, and execution of major projects. Giving change agents the proper tools—in the form of adequate communications—will ensure that they can serve the change initiative on an ongoing basis.

Communications: Create Once; Use Many Times

How do you help your formal leaders, when your change initiative is probably not the first thing on their minds, so that they can then help foster change? The most common complaint people have—and the higher people climb up the corporate ladder, the worse it is—is that they are too busy.

If you send your leaders a data-dump of materials that they must study hard to understand, most won't bother to read it, much less pass it on in any sort of comprehensible way to their direct reports. No, if you want your leaders or employees to spend time communicating in support of your change efforts, do the "heavy lifting" for them. Wrap the information in a bow, and make it easy for them to digest. I've heard a crasser and perhaps more memorable description put another way: "Do what momma bird does for her babies. Chew up their food and spit it down their throats for them."

BE THEIR SOURCE SMART

Constantly create collateral for others to use. Let them count on you to feed them information. At a minimum, you MANAGING should regularly issue some form of "speaking points" to your stakeholder community. This can be as simple as an e-mail of bullet points.

Key Messages: Creating a Hot Deck

No manager has ever complained to me about being underworked. In today's busy marketplace, I advocate implementing as many technology "crutches" as you can to make your job easier.

One of the main technology aids you have at your disposal is the "hot deck."

A lot of companies use SharePoint, which in many configurations has a feature

Hot Deck A master set of PowerPoint slides, talking points, or key information to be replicated for multiple uses. KEY TERM

called Slide Library. The information you put in this workspace is accessible to anyone who has a login, so you need to make sure the most current data is there.

Why is a hot deck so important? First, it ensures accuracy and consistency among messages being delivered. Second, a manager never has time to craft new messages or biweekly speaking points; this process makes it easy. Managers can pull current slides and customize them for meetings or presentations. Think of a hot deck as your communications first aid kit!

Make Sure Help Is in Place

So let's wrap it up. You can't do change by yourself; you will need help. The help you need is created by a leadership group that is completely aligned, regularly followed up with, and equipped with the latest and greatest information in an easy-to-find location. Even when all that fails, you still will have a Plan B in the form of well-respected people in the organization who capably and informally network the positive messages of your program. The key to making this all work is careful planning—making sure that help is in place well before you need it.

Manager's Checklist for Chapter 9

☑ Your "fulcrum" in a change initiative is the point around which you pivot the organization. The "lever" is the group of resources (like time, budget, and staff) you use to move the organization. Creating leverage lets you stretch and create resources where none have been provided—lengthening the lever.

☑ Leadership alignment is key to leverage. Ensure that your sponsor, executive sponsor, steering committee, and stakeholders are aligned in the message they tell—and that they tell it visibly and clearly for employees to hear.

☑ Stakeholder management involves identifying, analyzing, and engaging stakeholders.

☑ A change agent network catalyzes the change, improves the process, secures top-notch resources, and engages others in pivotal roles through your change initiative—even when you are busy.

☑ To ensure that your message sticks, create communications—such as a hot deck—that you create once and can use many times.

Measuring the Progress of Change

One of the great mistakes is to judge policies and programs by their intentions rather than their results.

—Milton Friedman

In my first week of work after graduating from college, my manager told me, "People will respect what is inspected." He proceeded to inform me of the exact criteria that he would use to measure my performance. I remember them clearly: "Make 10 sales calls and build displays of our products in three retail stores every day." I had to complete and submit a daily call report to track my performance. I knew what he was going to discuss with me every week: my adherence to these criteria and progress in achieving even higher levels of results.

I didn't realize it at the time, but having to adhere to the discipline of measuring and monitoring performance was not only a performance-tracking tool, but a change-management tool as well. The change required in this case was transforming a raw college student into a mature member of the workforce! I was changing because somebody was measuring me.

I've since come to understand that measurement is the secret weapon of change management. It's why measurement is a key strategy in the change plan I mentioned in Chapter 5. Here are three reasons why:

1. Only by inspecting performance can you ensure that your fellow change agents are implementing the initiatives you planned.

2. Only by inspecting performance can you tell what parts of the plan are going smoothly and which parts need help.

3. Only by inspecting performance can you ensure that the organization is making forward progress.

SMART

MANAGING

ESTABLISH MEASUREMENT CRITERIA UP FRONT

Why is measurement so important? Until you have reached the specific objectives spelled out in the vision for change, you haven't succeeded with your project. If you haven't reached those objectives, these questions arise:

- Was it a realistic objective?
- Was it a good, workable plan to achieve the objective?
- Did the execution of the plan occur as expected?

Having a well-documented measurement plan allows you to talk about the quality of the plan and whether the organization executed the change according to plan.

With the information and tactics provided in this chapter, you will gain the tools to monitor the execution of your change plan and drive progress. I explain how to identify milestones, assign responsibilities, set target dates, and summarize the results onto a scorecard where color-coding instantly communicates progress. When you're done with this chapter, you and your change sponsor will have the means to hold people accountable as they change from their current to future state.

Creating Effective Milestones

You already know the end point of your change initiative, but that end point is months away. How do you know if you're on track to arrive at that end point on schedule? To know where you are, you need to measure progress by milestones. You will want to consider four key elements of the milestone-setting process:

1. Defining the expected outcomes
2. Identifying who is accountable for ensuring each outcome is achieved
3. Providing a clear explanation of the outcome
4. Determining the dates the outcome is expected

We're now going to explain the concept of measurement as it applies to implementing an information technology project and the concept of "super users" we introduced in Chapter 9.

> **Milestone** A desired result that represents the achievement of a significant stage or completion of a step in a project. The term comes from the practice of placing stones or posts along a route to mark the distance in miles from place to place. **KEY TERM**

As we discussed, many large-scale systems projects rely on super users to provide peer-to-peer user support. Super users help other users become productive in the new system as quickly as possible. As part of your leverage strategy, your change plan engaged these respected individuals early in the project for input on the new system design. Now, as you move toward "go-live," these same people will deliver training to their peers. Note: the super user discussion is just an example. These measuring concepts apply to all change initiatives.

Defining the Expected Outcomes

To define milestones for your project, identify the various outcomes you should see as the project progresses; then write short descriptions of those outcomes. Having super users in place would certainly be a milestone in the path toward go-live. You might describe this milestone as simply, "Project sponsor certifies that super users are ready in all locations."

Obviously, "Project sponsor certifies that super users are ready in all locations" is a milestone along the way to the change. Super users don't just drop out of the sky, though. There are additional milestones along the way toward getting those super users ready. For example, you must:

- Identify super users
- Inform them of their responsibilities
- Relieve them of the appropriate amount of current workload
- Train them in the new systems

Once these steps are complete, the super users should report that they are prepared to support their fellow employees. The sponsor should be willing to "certify" that the work was completed to his or her satisfaction. *Identifying them, informing them, relieving them,* and *training them* are all smaller milestones on the way to the big milestone of *ensuring they are ready.*

I have two tips for defining milestones. Both require being specific:

1. **Determine how the milestone will be measured.** I frequently suggest using the term "Approved" or "Certified" to indicate that the milestone has been met, with specific instructions on who must provide this approval or what measurement is expected. Requiring specific approval steps makes it clear as to whether the milestone has been achieved. Doing so also ensures whoever is responsible for approving the relevant work takes ownership for seeing it through to timely completion.

2. **Quantify the result.** Beyond placing a person in charge of certifying the result, I also like to quantify the result. The way results are quantified varies. For example, notice in Table 10-1 that the first milestone, Super user network design approved," requires a simple yes or no answer. The super user network is either designed, or it isn't. To see if this milestone has been met, simply go to the vice president of HR on the due date and ask to see his or her approval on a document stating that this has been completed. The remaining four milestones on this table, however, are different. They must be expressed in varying numeric and percentage terms. For example, if you have designed a super user network of 50 people and managers have appointed only 20 so far, the task is 40 percent complete. Regardless of how your result is measured, it should be defined (and certified) in quantifiable terms.

WHY MEASUREMENT MATTERS TO ME, AND YOU

FOR EXAMPLE

When approaching change, the bias of a communications department might be to create more internal newsletters. The bias of a corporate psychologist might be to allow people to talk about the initiative and their reaction to it. The bias of HR might be to increase incentives. All these methods are valid and useful in managing change, but they all fail without solid measurement of the change effort's effectiveness.

My bias for measurement comes from my background as a sales manager. The only way to truly evaluate whether my sales team's efforts were working was to measure, measure, measure. The only way to evaluate your initiative's progress is to measure, measure, measure.

Assigning Responsibilities

The next step in milestone management is to assign responsibilities.

To publicly report progress, you need to "name names." Every milestone needs to have a person accountable for achieving the milestone.

Your milestone work can be summarized as shown in Table 10-1.

Milestone	Person Accountable
Super User Network Design Approved	VP of Human Resources
Super Users Appointed	Project Sponsor
Super Users Relieved of Current Responsibilities	Project Sponsor
Super Users Trained in the New System	Project Manager
Super Users Self-Report Readiness	VP of Human Resources

Table 10-1. Example milestones with accountabilities

THE FAMILY REUNION

To understand the importance and value of setting milestones and assigning responsibilities, consider planning a family reunion. Let's say that Grandma is in charge of the invites. Aunt Sally does menu planning. Uncle Billy does food prep coordination. Cousin Jim does the airport pickups. Cousin Titus is in charge of clean-up, etc.

Let's say everyone does his or her part except for Grandma. For some reason, she doesn't get around to inviting anyone. Will the reunion be a success? No.

This example also uses the theme from one of the first two chapters: *You already know how to do this because you use the skills at home.* This may seem like a silly example, but it's only silly because these processes seem simple when they pertain to personal goals. In your change effort, the milestones might seem more complex, but the lesson is still simple: if you don't clearly assign your milestones and communicate the objectives, you won't arrive at your destination with the results you want.

Clearly Defining Milestones

Providing a clear explanation of the desired outcomes by capturing the basic milestones and assigning responsibilities is a good start, but it isn't enough. To help a project go smoothly, everyone involved has to gain the same understanding of what the milestones mean. So the next step is a little harder: writing out a full, unambiguous definition of each milestone. Let's face it, an outcome like "Super users self-report readiness" could be interpreted many ways. The following sentence is much less open to misinterpretation:

> Super users will be surveyed five weeks and two weeks before go-live and asked if they are prepared to deliver necessary end-user training, are clear on the responsibilities of their positions, have been allotted sufficient time to support their peers, and are confident in their abilities to help their peers. 85 percent of super users must declare themselves ready to support their peers.

Writing clear definitions of each milestone, collaborating with individuals who are accountable for delivering the milestone, and making those milestones widely available are important for three reasons:

1. This level of clarity makes it difficult for "slicker" members of your project team to sidestep responsibilities.
2. Your executives will find it difficult to manage merely from the summary-level milestones. You must provide them with more specificity on the group's expectations.
3. Collaborating with the accountable individuals ensures they develop a sense of personal accountability for achieving the result.

TRICKS OF THE TRADE

BE BIASED TOWARD RESULTS

Measuring the number of activities that have occurred has a place in monitoring a change program, but only a small place. The Milton Friedman quote at the beginning of the chapter would even suggest that judging a program by its intent alone is a mistake. It is *results* that matter. In the super user example, for instance, knowing how many training classes have occurred isn't important. Holding a class is an *activity*. Having a super user certify that he or she is ready to train peers, however, is an outcome of an activity. It is a *result*.

While there may be times when an activity metric is helpful to gauge progress, make sure you're focused on how you will measure the results you are (or aren't) seeing. Sure, it's important to measure whether you have sent out the expected number of newsletters, but it's far more important to measure whether doing so resulted in the desired level of awareness.

Establishing Due Dates

At this point, you have built a list of milestones, assigned responsibilities, and specified in a few sentences the full meaning of the milestone.

The milestones will measure how far you have traveled. Your milestones will also tell you the schedule you are following. As you build your plan, you will need to establish a date by which the milestones must be achieved. You will evaluate progress against those dates as you work through the project. Using the super-user example, assigning dates can be as simple as shown in Table 10-2.

Milestone	Due Date
Super User Network Design Approved	February 1
Super Users Appointed	April 1
Super Users Relieved of Current Responsibilities	April 30
Super Users Trained in the New System	June 30
Super Users Self-Report Readiness	July 15

Table 10-2. Example project milestones and due dates

Judging Progress

Later in this chapter, we review ways to communicate the status of milestones, but first we need to discuss your responsibilities as a change agent to ensure that accountable people or groups are carrying out their assigned tasks.

This can get tricky, especially since it's likely some of the accountable people will be higher than you in the corporate hierarchy.

COLLABORATE IN SETTING DUE DATES

TRICKS OF THE TRADE

When establishing due dates, it's important to do so in collaboration with the people who are accountable for achieving the milestones. When they commit to the dates, you'll be holding them to their commitments—not to the dates that you thought were good ones. This process is more effective when the responsible people agree to the date.

Managing Up

In our super-user scenario, would it be appropriate for you to go to the project sponsor—even if this person is your senior leader—and ask if all the super users have been appointed yet? Is it appropriate to ask for the list of super users by name? My answer is simple: absolutely! When you identified who was accountable for each milestone, you set the expectation for follow-up.

Several people I have coached through this process have been apprehensive about evaluating whether a senior executive has completed a task. In short, don't worry. Here's why:

- **The executive wants to lead by example.** The executive knows something you may not realize yet: he wants to achieve his milestone on time so he can say to the rest of the project team, "I got mine done; why can't you get yours done?"
- **You can leverage the executive leader's buy-in.** By checking in with the executive, you gain the opportunity to invoke her name throughout the course of the project, thus creating the case for buy-in from other team members: "When I was working with our senior vice president, Mary, on her part of the project, she believed firmly in delivering on time."
- **You foster a key relationship with the senior leadership.** You probably will have a positive experience with the executive. Job titles rarely matter when individuals are trying something out of their comfort zones. An executive is apt to ask you the same questions as anyone else, looking for your guidance and treating you as the expert as he works on his area of responsibility. This gives you a chance to create or strengthen a key relationship with the senior leader.

If you experience an executive unwilling to follow through on his or her commitments, work with the project sponsor on the best course of action for remedying this situation. Remember, you're the change manager. You own the quality of the change plan and, therefore, the reporting on the status of activities. The project sponsor—the person ultimately accountable for the project's success—will need to handle the nonperforming executive to ensure success.

Managing Shared Responsibilities

Although you may have named a single point of accountability for each of your milestones, many people likely will contribute to the activity's completion. In our scenario, think about the super users named. Do you have super users named in the finance function? How about in the manufacturing function? How about in marketing? Many people will contribute to the finished project, and you must ensure that the person accountable for the finished state is tracking progress in each subarea.

I've constructed a small tracking spreadsheet as an example of how to track progress across several areas (see Table 10-3).

Super Users Needed In	Finance		Manufacturing		Marketing	
	Number	Percent	Number	Percent	Number	Percent
Design Document	8		20		14	
Super Users Appointed	8	100%	20	100%	10	77%
Super Users with Current Responsibilities Relieved	7		20	100%	10	71%
Super Users Trained	6	88%	20	100%	10	71%
Super Users with Self-Reported Readiness	5	67%	10	50%	10	71%

Table 10-3. Progress tracking

From this sample spreadsheet, it's clear that, while progress has been made, none of the areas have met the requirements completely yet. The finance group's execution seems to have faded as the project progresses. That group started by assigning roles properly but lost participation at every milestone since that time. Manufacturing has done exactly what it was supposed to do but still has some work in getting its super users ready. Marketing has executed a plan perfectly, but the plan will give its group an inadequate number of super users. Analyzing this level of data gives senior management and you the opportunity to take action.

Building Your Scorecard

Once you've developed all the pieces described—milestones, accountable people, supporting documentation, target dates—summarize the results in a scorecard. Simply lay out a table showing all milestones in all categories, then assign colors to each cell in the table that signal the status of

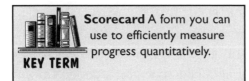

Scorecard A form you can use to efficiently measure progress quantitatively.

KEY TERM

that item. The purpose of this scorecard is to help you monitor progress and outcomes on each crucial element of your plan.

What Goes on the Scorecard?

If the change you're leading is a simple one, it's okay to use a simple grid like that shown for the super users earlier in this chapter. In most major changes, though, you need a more sophisticated scorecard with more detail about what needs to be accomplished for the change to occur on time, on budget, and with the desired results.

What goes on the scorecard? The answer is "your milestones." Though every change initiative has a unique path to success, many commonalities exist. The first milestone to be achieved on any change initiative is typically something along the lines of "Vision Established, Sponsor Named, and Resources Allocated." If you don't yet know where you're going, who will lead the change, and what initial resources you'll use to get going, you aren't ready to start—which is why this serves as a solid example of a typical first milestone.

The last milestone is frequently "Project Team Reassigned." Your team may consist of only you, or it may be a huge group. In any case, the

BE OPEN ABOUT SCORECARDING PROCESS

It has been my experience that organizations that use a scorecard approach to track progress toward organization readiness focus on the scorecard. That is good for the person administering the scorecard, but it also exerts pressure. Some people will want the progress evaluation to be "generous" in their favor. While this might be helpful to those people, it hurts your project—and you in the long term.

My advice: Have your sponsor state publicly, "I'm asking my change management person to administer a scorecard measuring our progress. I expect him or her to give me an unbiased view of our progress. If I don't have that view, I won't be in a position to help those who need help."

By saying this, you create some cover. You can now say, "I can't mark that milestone complete because it really isn't done. If we give a correct reading, that will encourage leadership to give you the resources you need to be successful."

team needs to be moved on to their next assignment. The project isn't over until you hit this milestone.

To start building your own scorecard, look at the plan you have developed. The activities likely fall into categories such as:

1. **Critical Success Factors.** Activities that build a foundation for success (such as getting senior staff to agree on a vision, developing new policies to support the desired change, and developing a risk management plan)
2. **Leadership Readiness.** Activities that ensure the right leadership with the right skills is in place to drive the change
3. **Work/Organization Design.** Activities that replace the "old ways" of doing business with descriptions of the "new ways" (new processes, procedures, roles/responsibilities, work groups)
4. **Employee Readiness and Training/Education.** Activities that prepare employees to succeed during and after the change (including job training, logistics of the training/education programs)
5. **Business Readiness.** Activities that prepare the business as a whole for the change—including communication plans, launch plans, and post-change operational plans
6. **Post-Launch Support.** Activities that develop users' ability to get implementation help after the launch
7. **Transition Plan.** Activities that wrap up all change activities, including the transfer of any ongoing responsibilities, and reassignment of the change team (if needed)

Your plan may create other categories, such as communication/education with customers or third party/supplier preparation if the change will affect people beyond your company's boundaries. Alternately, not all the categories here may be relevant for your change effort (a reorganization, for example, may not require any training).

Within each category, summarize the milestones for that category to be considered complete and successful. Label the columns of a spreadsheet or table with these categories. Then in each category, identify the:

- What (milestone)
- Who (accountable person)

> **TWO EXAMPLES OF ADDITIONAL CATEGORIES**
>
> One company I worked with was implementing a change to create a universal process across an organization that had been run as independent silos for years. A big part of the change plan involved creating "cultural readiness." Leaders planned to implement activities to build understanding of why the new system would be better for the business and, ultimately, for its managers and executives. Since the change involved another organization bringing in a new data system that few managers were familiar with, one of the categories created was "management team education," which included activities like training for all top leaders, observation of the system in use in another company, and discussion among key leaders of what implementation would mean for the company.

■ When (due date) for each activity

Table 10-4, for example, shows the first two categories (Critical Success Factors and Leadership Readiness) and first two milestones in those categories for a systems implementation plan.

	A Critical Success Factors	B Leadership Readiness
1	Vision, Sponsorship, and Resources Established	Plant Champions Named
	9/5/12 Greg	11/13/12 Marcia
2	Senior Staff Agrees to Objectives and Approach	Leadership Education Completed
	9/5/12 Greg	12/1/12 DeWayne

Table 10-4. Sample scorecard

The structure of the table in Table 10-4 is important because it gives you a simple *letter + number* shorthand for identifying the cells in the table (A1, B12, etc.). Don't worry about the number of boxes. The largest number of milestones I've managed was 56. The smallest was 9. This scorecard approach is scalable to the size of the initiative.

USING THE SUPPORTING DETAIL

SMART

MANAGING

Earlier in the chapter, I advised you to write a detailed description of each milestone. Once you have created the scorecard, you can label each definition according to its corresponding cell. You can't expect the people implementing the plan to have your same level of familiarity with the details. I guarantee that anyone not involved full-time in the change likely will forget the details. Providing people with backup information linked to a specific spot on the scorecard will help them understand what they must hold others accountable for. If using Table 10-4, for example, providing a document labeled B2 to define the milestone of "leadership education completed" would add clarity to this point.

Using the Scorecard to Monitor and Manage

Scorecards are useful only if they are *simple to understand and use.* Because most change efforts involve many distinct pieces, I personally experience great success with a "checkerboard" approach—using a simple color code. Here is what I mean:

Once you create a chart like that shown in Table 10-4 (with actions, names, and due dates), meet with each accountable person every week. I recommend adjusting the colors based on progress:

- If the accountable person is on track to reach the milestone on time, leave the box white.
- If the accountable person has reached the milestone, turn the box green.
- If the accountable person is going to be late, turn the box yellow.
- If the accountable person misses the deadline, turn the box red.

The result is a simple visual representation of what must be achieved, who's accountable for delivering the result, and whether the result will be achieved on time. Your main goal is to determine when and how to intervene, if

PAY ATTENTION TO YOUR COMPANY'S COLOR SCHEME

SMART

MANAGING

I've worked in companies where red meant "going poorly," yellow meant "we are struggling," and green meant "all is good." The color scheme that I laid out here communicated a different set of messages. It may be helpful for you to include a legend on the bottom of your scorecard to communicate exactly what your colors indicate.

DAILY CHECK-IN

When I'm managing a change effort, I try to have regular meetings or conference calls with all key staff wherein they report their status using a 1–5 scale: 1 means "I'm okay," and 5 means "I need help." Doing this helps me allocate my time most wisely. If the effort is fast-paced, I recommend holding these quick check-ins daily.

necessary, to keep the effort on track. Seeing that there are tasks in yellow or red says you can talk to the people in charge of these tasks to find out what's holding them back or preventing them from completing their tasks.

As you meet with those accountable for each milestone, take notes in the scorecard document. Add notes every week that you meet with these key players, and you will create a journal of the commitments made through the course of the initiative. Documentation of previous conversations has been my friend on several occasions.

Being Proactive with the Yellows and Reds

The individuals accountable for reaching milestones do not like having a missed or potentially missed milestone made public by receiving yellow or red designations on the scorecard. They often argue they are on track to reach the milestones on time or that they have reached milestones when they really haven't. A vice president at one of my clients' companies, for example, argued with me that the milestone titled "Forecast the Training Resources" was achieved because he'd estimated that the project would require 2,000 hours of training. If I had accepted his

KNOW WHEN TO TRACK PROGRESS AND WHEN TO BACK OFF

The more granular you become in tracking progress, the less risk you experience in slipping seriously behind. Going back to my experience after college, my boss talked to me every day during the first month. He then moved to talking to me every week. The better I became, the less we needed to talk about my performance. He learned to trust that I was delivering. You will need to strike that same balance. Everybody who is contributing to your project will have his or her progress tracked. You will need to track some progress more closely than other progress.

definition of complete, the client would have known how many trainers to secure in total, but not how many by location. So that task was not complete.

The best way to avoid these arguments is to specifically define the tasks in the backup materials previously discussed—such as the descriptions of the milestones and who is responsible for them. In this case, I was fortunate that I had been specific in the backup material. I pointed out that he hadn't met the real criteria for completion: identifying how many employees would be trained by shift, by location, and by class. The task wasn't complete until the subtasks were complete according to the predefined criteria.

You will want your scorecard to honestly and accurately depict the status of each milestone. You will only achieve an honest, reliable record if people understand that the status will be used to help them. Don't use a late milestone to create shame. If people are falling behind, find a way to get them additional resources. Use milestone measurements to create success.

If the scorecard doesn't accurately represent reality, your ability to manage is compromised. Don't give in to pressure to avoid the yellows or reds.

> **OVERCOMING THE FEAR OF RED**
>
> Part of the reason people fear having their tasks labeled as red or bad numbers reported on a scorecard is due to a fear that documentation of poor performance will be used against them—perhaps through the loss of a raise or promotion. It's critical that you show by your behavior that the scorecard (and reporting results) will be used to manage the change, not punish the changers.

Will Scorecards Work for You?

In general, measurement-driven implementation provides the greatest value in organizations when the culture has strong senior leadership with a track record of holding people accountable for results. People in these organizations expect their performance to be publicly reported. Senior leadership desires to go from Point A to Point C, and you can serve as the scorekeeper along the way.

EXPOSING RESISTANCE BY "SHINING A LIGHT ON IT"

I have a philosophy in change management regarding resistance. That is, when I have a resister, my typical tactic is to shine a light on the resistance. Don't undermine the resister or send him more newsletters, etc. Instead, shine the light on the source of resistance. Ask him or her honestly how it is going. Then, determine how this person's resistance fits into the guiding principles of your company or change initiative. If you shine a light on the issue, rather than stuffing it in the closet, you not only gain the opportunity to break through resistance more quickly—you also foster a culture of trust and participation. When in doubt, get the issues out in the open.

Measurement also works wonders in highly competitive organizations. One client I worked with posted the scorecard for each vice president's area of responsibility in the cafeteria for each employee to see. Employees clearly understood the activities occurring on the project and how each function was progressing. In a way, this approach is no different than placing stars on a six-year-old's refrigerator chart. You're communicating what's expected and recognizing when expectations are met.

Not every organization's culture supports such a public communication of performance. In such an environment, the cafeteria communication would almost certainly backfire. Although you still need to measure progress, how results are communicated in such a culture changes. There will be resistance from middle management, but your job still is to work around that resistance.

Six Elements for Measuring Progress

To summarize the concepts introduced in this chapter, if you put the following six elements in place, your scorecard will be a success:

1. Senior-level sponsorship and participation in the scorecard process
2. Clear and unambiguous definitions of expectations
3. Due dates for each milestone
4. The person accountable for achieving each milestone
5. An objective scorekeeper with the courage to report when senior individuals fall behind
6. A regular process to gather and report status

Good Leadership = Good Scorecards

One leader I worked with took it upon himself to become the "communicator-in-chief." He knew the message would get muddled and watered down as it cascaded through middle management. So he called in every super user on a systems

> ### INTEGRATE ALL LEVELS OF THE SCORECARD
>
>
>
> SMART
>
> MANAGING
>
> My best advice for reviewing the scorecard is to integrate, integrate, integrate. Make sure the plan makes sense *as a whole*—that there aren't any conflicts in the activities or timing of activities in different categories. As an obvious example, you can't "go live" before training is complete or before a pilot test is done (if relevant).

implementation project and delivered the following message: "You are critical to making us successful. Please accept this certificate of my thanks for your efforts. Please display it for all to see. You will play a vital role in helping your peers. We have no greater objective than ensuring every employee in this organization is highly productive. Only you can make that happen." Trust me—middle management resistance stopped.

I firmly believe that a good scorecard used well is critical to effective change management. But as you've seen, anticipate some resistance and fear, especially if your organization hasn't used anything like this before.

Leaders need to communicate to all frontline employees and managers that having a *scorecard reflecting reality* is essential for good change management. They also need to make it okay for people to self-report a yellow or red status and to ask for help when needed. Create an accepted standard that if someone isn't going to make a deadline, it's best—both for the individual and the business—if this person admits it won't be met.

When it comes to scorecards, it doesn't matter whether you're running an enterprise, functional, site-specific, or team change initiative. You need to know your milestones, target dates for completion, and how you will measure progress and results quantitatively and/or qualitatively. This capability will give you the best chance for success.

Manager's Checklist for Chapter 10

☑ Measurement is key because it allows you to quantify the results of your change efforts.

☑ Creating effective and clearly defined and assigned milestones will enable you to track and accomplish your goals in manageable "chunks."

☑ Involve your senior leadership appropriately to foster buy-in and build relationships.

☑ Use scorecards to assess where you are (what, who, and when) in the key milestones.

☑ Expect conflict, and don't let it paralyze your measurement process.

The Secret Weapon: Governance

Governance and leadership are the yin and the yang of successful organizations. If you have leadership without governance you risk tyranny, fraud, and personal fiefdoms. If you have governance without leadership you risk atrophy, bureaucracy, and indifference.

—Mark Goyder, Director of Tomorrow's Company

L eft to their own devices, people will do what they think is best for themselves. Leaders therefore need to guide people to do the right things at the right times—and rules need to be set to ensure everything works within the organization. Without strong leaders and clear rules, bedlam ensues. I've seen it happen!

The first example of a bedlam environment comes about from a reduced sense of *personal accountability*. In this type of organization, employees don't feel empowered or motivated to make decisions or take action for anything beyond the here and now. This type of company has vice presidents who don't think in terms of what's best for the enterprise. These VPs think of what's best only for their own functions. This type of organization needs a set of rules and strong leadership to create a shift toward enterprise-wide thinking.

In a company I recently worked with, we followed all the suggestions laid out in this book. We paid close attention to laying out clear roles and responsibility definitions. Subject matter experts were expected to create designs and deliver them to the sponsor and steering committee by a cer-

THINKING BEYOND ONE'S FUNCTION

Imagine a CFO who wants to work on increasing cash flow: "Get paid faster." The CFO is thinking in enterprise-wide terms. Let's say you're charged with addressing this challenge. You may go to the accounts receivable department and find out it spends a lot of time chasing customers because the invoices are incorrect. You realize that if the invoices were correct, the company would get paid faster and increase its cash flow.

The AR group doesn't want to fix the invoices, though, because that is the responsibility of the customer service department. You find out the customer service department has lots of issues with sending out incorrect invoices, but the group's success is measured on getting invoices out quickly, not correctly. Customer service, however, claims the issue with poor invoice quality is due to the sales force handing in purchase orders without checking their work; the salespeople don't want to spend time on the issue because they get paid on sales volume, not cash flow.

This organization needs to authorize an individual to work across functions, even if only for a short time, to take action in areas outside of his or her traditional control.

tain date. When that date came, so did the excuses: "We were too busy." "It was too hard." "We had higher priorities." The list was long. In response, the sponsor extended the due date and reduced the scope of what was to be delivered. There was no admonishment or expression of disappointment.

Interestingly, about a month later it came time for this company to name super users to support the initiative. The sponsor stated, "Last time we named subject matter experts to be accountable for a body of work, and that didn't work out too well. This time, instead of assigning work, we should ask for volunteers." This brings to mind the quote, "The lunatics are running the asylum" (with no offense meant to lunatics or asylum managers). How will this organization ever change if the person responsible for the change won't insist on change? This organization suffered from *a failure of leadership*.

Rules and enforcement are vital when both leaders *and* employees are strong-minded. When employees feel they have the right to do as they see fit, the organization experiences a *culture of entitlement*.

A company president told me a story that illustrated an example of this type of culture. Immediately following the 9/11 attacks—when a huge outpouring of American patriotism and support existed for the first responders—this company's marketing organization responded by recommending that it change the color scheme of its product to red, white, and blue. With every sale of this special edition product, the company would make a donation to various first responder

> **A ROLE OF THE STEERING COMMITTEE**
>
> In a properly functioning organization, the steering committee should have their responsibilities defined in such a way that they see the sponsor's leadership failure. The steering committee should actually own the results of the sponsor's work and be willing to adjust if leadership is falling short.

charity organizations. The president issued the direction: do it immediately.

Two weeks passed. Nothing happened. Employees actually ignored the directive given to them. They chose to work on something else. The president fumed and then issued a company-wide e-mail: "If anybody has a reason why we shouldn't move forward with this project, come to XYZ conference room at such and such a time." In a sense, he had issued a challenge. In my high school, this was "calling somebody out." There was going to be a fight at the bridge behind the school right after classes.

To his amazement, more than a dozen people showed up. He told me, "There were people I didn't even recognize, and that meant they had to be

> **THE BIGGER PICTURE**
>
> **SMART MANAGING**
>
> As a change manager, you may find there are larger dynamics at play than the immediate change on the table. The client with an overly entitled workforce was a perfect example. While I was worried about the changes related to a reorganization, the president was worried about a culture that was impeding growth. He knew that he needed to force employees to respond—but to respond productively and appropriately. So over the next couple of years, the president replaced 80 percent of his direct reports. His rationale was "Until I had at least half of my management team prepared to address the cultural issues surrounding the sense of entitlement and lack of response, change management would be a waste. There would be no change in this organization until the organization would respond when directed."
>
> My short-term reorganization project was a success, but only because we weren't taking on large changes. The bigger changes this company took on came in the years after the direct reports were changed.

at least three levels down from me. Imagine the brain that says it is going to go tell the president 'no.'" He was amazed that people felt they had the right to challenge his decision. The employees felt empowered to ignore the president and then publicly tell him "no."

As a change manager, you need to know how to use governance *to ensure that people do what they need to do.* You may not be completely successful, but the rules that governance creates give you the best possible chance to succeed. In this chapter, we discuss how to use governance to enhance and protect your change efforts by addressing potential culture and performance issues before they become problems.

> **KEY TERM** **Governance** Wikipedia defines governance as "decisions that define *expectations*, grant power, or verify performance." In business, this involves "consistent management, cohesive policies, guidance, processes, and decision-rights for a given area of responsibility."

Elements That Guide Governance

There are many elements that guide governance. For the purpose of this book, I outline six elements that should ensure you have systems in place to proactively circumvent or address any culture or performance issues you may encounter. These six elements are:

1. **Establish objectives.** Your expectations are synonymous with your objectives. *Tell your people what you want from them.*
2. **Create guiding principles.** Your guiding principles are your overarching beliefs that tell people how you will make decisions—pulling people through your vision to your goal. Change initiatives are loaded with imperfect information at the start. The only thing you have is the ability to clarify the criteria that will guide your decision making. *Tell employees what they need to do to ensure goals are achieved.*
3. **Grant authority and responsiblity in relationships.** Ensure that your people are clear on their roles and responsibilities, including the chain of command—and give them authority to act appropriately. *Make it clear to employees who is doing what and who they report to.*

4. **Verify performance.** We discussed the need for measurement. I learned early in my career that people respect what is inspected. *Tell your employees how they're doing in meeting their milestones.*

5. **Institute cohesive ways of working.** Your policies or rules should cover how you communicate to your project team, deal with management issues, and deal with management risks. *Provide specifics on how the organization will operate as the change is implemented.*

6. **Foster a culture of collaboration.** Change is hard. We've already reviewed the need for participa-

> ### WHY GOVERNANCE IS A GROUP EFFORT
> **TRICKS OF THE TRADE**
>
> You may wonder why I am suggesting that change management has a role in governance. You might believe that governance is the sponsor's job or the project manager's job. You're right—it is their job. But you are a big stakeholder in ensuring that governance is implemented, and implemented well. You'll be ineffective without it. So as the sponsors or project managers are shaping their program, you need to be at the table to help shape the governance program.

tion. The best project team culture is one of collaboration. Collaboration invests everybody in the outcome. *Show your employees how to act, and empower them to do their jobs.*

We will go into more depth on these six elements throughout the rest of this chapter.

Key Elements #1 and #2: Establish Objectives and Guiding Principles

One of the most important elements in governance involves making sure your objectives are clearly thought out, defined, and communicated. Your objectives should include the quantitative and qualitative aspects that signal you are reaching your vision. As discussed in Chapter 3, your objectives should be SMART: Strategic and Specific, Measurable, Attainable, Results-oriented, and Time-bound.

To do so, you need to reintroduce your definition of success. Ensure your managers clearly spell out what success looks like—quantitatively and qualitatively. That definition of success is your guiding light. It also means that when you have trouble in the project and need help, you can go to your managers and say, "I am trying to get to X, and to get there, I need Y." A clear definition of success helps you gain commitment from managers and employees and ensures they are actively invested in that success.

Once the change objectives are defined, ensure they are supported by clear *guiding principles*. Closely tied to corporate core values, guiding principles shape the decisions about the unknowns you will encounter on the project. Your company may have organizational guiding principles already in place. If so, you will need to apply them to the change initiative. The sidebar (below) provides an example of one company's guiding principles.

MARS' FIVE CORE PRINCIPLES

FOR EXAMPLE

Below are the guiding principles for Mars, Inc. (Think M&Ms and Snickers bars.)

1. **Quality:** Quality is the first ingredient of quality brands. The consumer is our boss. Quality is our work, and delivering value for money is our goal.
2. **Responsibility:** All associates are asked to take direct responsibility for results, to exercise initiative and judgment, and to make decisions as required.
3. **Mutuality:** A mutual benefit is a shared benefit, and a shared benefit will endure.
4. **Efficiency:** Use resources to the full capacity, waste nothing, and do only what we can do best in order to maximize productivity.
5. **Freedom:** We need freedom to shape our future and profit to remain free. Family ownership was a deliberate choice.

Source: www.mars.com/global/about-mars/the-five-principles-of-mars.aspx

---

Taking time to align your guiding principles with your specific change will serve you well and keep your people clear on what you expect. Most don't think of this process as governance. Your typical project management book doesn't push this concept. But change initiatives are about following a leader to a new place. People follow principled leaders through thick and thin. State your principles, and follow them. Your employees will be more willing to endure hardship when they see a leader make a tough call based on principles, rather than when he or she reacts based on emotion.

Your guiding principles should tell people how you make decisions. I have seen guiding principles about such things as:

AGREE ON PRIORITIES

I once entered a project midway and asked people about the guiding principles shaping their decisions. Unfortunately, there were three different documents floating around—each providing different direction. We had to bring everybody together and reach an agreement: What is our number one priority? What is number two? Once we gained agreement on priorities, the project team worked much more efficiently and productively.

- Protecting an investment already made in a system (e.g., "We aren't throwing the current system out").
- How jobs will be arranged (e.g., "If we have job location changes, people will need to be based in the location of the new job").
- Ratio of workers to managers. (Although it sounds like a goal, it was actually a guiding principle in a cost-cutting project. We needed to know where to cut—in this case, managers.)

Make sure your guiding principles address the following questions: How do you want the change to be run? What are your priorities as you move through the project? What can people count on you to do? One good example principle: "We will communicate when we have reached a decision and have a plan to deal with the implications. If we haven't made a decision within a certain time frame, we will inform you of that and when we will have a decision." Believe it or not, this simple statement

MUST-HAVE GUIDING PRINCIPLE:
PRIORITIZATION OF QUALITY, COST, AND TIME

SMART

MANAGING

Your guiding principles may take many forms, but an important principle to consider is the priority of quality, cost, and time. It's important for leaders to state their order of priority. Often, a project team will get in a jam. When this happens, one of these three priorities may be compromised. Team members need to know which of these priorities management is most willing to concede. By defining your priorities up front, before you run into trouble, you will have a road map for getting through the jam.

enabled people not to worry constantly that there was *secret* news that hadn't been disclosed.

It's critical to communicate your project's guiding principles to anybody who might be impacted by your initiative.

Key Element #3: Grant Authority and Responsibility in Relationships

We've discussed various roles in previous chapters. As they pertain to governance, this section provides some fine tuning on how you can use roles to your advantage in the change process by granting the proper authority and responsibility in the relationships you manage. People need to understand who gets to make what kinds of decisions. It's pretty clear from the work we did in the last chapter that the person who makes the final decision on each of the milestones will be the person accountable for that "box" on the scorecard.

Implement RACI

RACI is an acronym that defines how your people will carry out their roles. It hints at the underlying purpose of each role and, in this way, is loosely tied to governing principles. RACI stands for:

Responsible: Those who conduct the actual task. Typically, there is one individual who is the person *responsible* for the task, while you may have others assigned to assist in this role.

Accountable (also *approver* or final *approving authority*): This is whom the *responsible* role reports to in order to ensure the task is completely and correctly delivered. The person *accountable* approves the work done by those *responsible*. There should be one person *accountable* for each deliverable task.

Consulted (sometimes *counsel*): This is a role whose input and opinions others pay attention to. Often this is a stakeholder with whom two-way communication is imperative.

Informed: The person in this role is kept abreast of progress, particularly when a task is completed. Typically, this role requires only one-way communication.

Use RAPID Decision Making

TRICKS OF THE TRADE

Another way to set up good decision-making protocols can be found in the often-used acronym RAPID, which stands for:

Recommender—The person who starts the process and makes sure people are clear on what they must do and that they are moving ahead.

Agree or Approve—The person who must sign off on a decision. This person has more authority than an "I."

Perform—This person executes the decision once it is made.

Input—The person who is consulted before making a decision, but who does not vote on the outcome.

Decide—This person or group has final and ultimate authority.

Clarify who fits into which roles within the RAPID framework.

(RAPID is a service mark of Bain & Company, Inc.)

Sometimes the person in the *accountable* role for a deliverable is also *responsible* for finishing it. Beyond this exception, I recommend that different people take on each of the RACI roles. Otherwise, it may mean that you have not fully resolved or defined these roles, which can take away from your ability to use RACI to its full advantage.

Make Sure Roles and Responsibilities Are Clear

To ensure that people properly act on their authority—without developing an undue sense of entitlement—it's important to make sure roles and responsibilities are clear. Make sure the process and the change management people know what they're supposed to do and when they're supposed to do it. And make sure they are empowered to do their jobs.

Empower To equip someone with the power and motivation to act influentially. An empowered **KEY TERM** employee has specific responsibility for his or her tasks and does not need approval to do what needs to be done.

Put the Change Manager in the Optimal Spot in the Reporting Chain

So who should the change manager report to?

One common question in an IT-related change is whether the change manager should report to the IT department. Let's explore this.

KEEPING IT SMOOTH
Too often a change project works like a whip. A slow motion move at one end causes major impacts at the other end. It takes coordination and collaboration to ensure this doesn't happen. As the change manager, you are frequently at the end of the whip. Design and building can take a long time, and you are expected to work miracles in a limited amount of time at the end of the project for things like training. Insist that you are at the table as the master timeline is assembled.

In thinking about an IT-oriented change initiative, a natural tension exists between organizational objectives. The information technology group typically is driven by objectives such as cost, project timelines, and information security while meeting the needs of its internal clients. Those internal clients—frequently the owners of a particular business process—place a lower value on IT's objectives. Process owners are most concerned about employee effectiveness and efficiency. Process owners frequently trade short-term costs for long-term productivity gains, something that can be at odds with the IT department's objectives.

In thinking about typical organizational change managers and their work, it's clear that they are most closely aligned with the process owner. They want the long-term change to be effective and are less concerned with the short-term costs or the process of implementing the change than they are with the result. It follows that having the change manager report

WORKING WITH HR
It's common for a change manager to report to the HR department. HR can be an effective advisor to a senior manager—or it can be a group whose business judgment isn't well respected. If you are to be an effective change manager, you must meet the sponsor's needs. Your secondary responsibility is to a staff function, such as IT or HR.

to the IT organization, for example, misaligns interests. It becomes too easy for the cost-and-time-driven IT manager to stifle input from the change management team.

This is particularly true if the project manager can overrule the input of the change manager and does not allow for an independent line of communication with the leader. In other words, it makes more sense for the change manager to have a direct reporting relationship to the business sponsor accountable for the project's success. Granted, the sponsor typically doesn't want multiple project direct reports, but it has been my experience that a sponsor will be more interested in talking about business and organizational issues than the status of IT topics, such as integration testing and data cleansing routines. The sponsor needs to play an active role in leading the project and needs to be current on the business and organization issues being caused or cured by the change project.

Key Element #4: Verify Performance

We already covered measurement extensively in Chapter 10. For the purposes of this chapter, understand that creating systems to verify performance at various milestones is a crucial part of governance.

An important measurement tool you may want to implement is an *Organization Readiness Survey*, which assesses how key players feel about the change, their view on how ready the organization is to engage in the changes, and their perceptions of the impact the change may have on employees and customers. Such a survey may help you identify gaps where readiness doesn't exist—such as communication gaps—so you'll know where to focus your training. As it pertains to the example that opened the chapter, this survey can help you identify key culture issues before they become problems. On the next page you will find a sample Organization Readiness Survey.

> ### What If My Organization Is Not Ready?   TRICKS OF THE TRADE
> I have worked with people new to the field of change management who found it odd that I suggested an Organization Readiness Survey. Their logic was that if the organization reports that it isn't ready, won't that reflect poorly on the change manager? Well perhaps, but by this point you should be thinking that organizational change management is a group effort. Many people own pieces of helping an organization change. You are a facilitator and coordinator of work occurring in lots of places. It isn't about what you as the change manager can accomplish. It is about what the organization does accomplish.

SAMPLE ORGANIZATION READINESS SURVEY

1. In which business area do you work? (select from a list of your departments)

2. At which location do you work? (select from a list)

3. What level are you in the organization? (executive, VP, director, manager, supervisor, frontline team member)

Please rate how much you agree with each of the statements below by marking an X in the column that best represents your view.

	Strongly Agree	Agree	Disagree	Strongly Disagree	N/A
1. I have heard of the change project.	❏	❏	❏	❏	❏
2. I am familiar with the planned timing for the project.	❏	❏	❏	❏	❏
3. I understand how the project will affect my day-to-day work.	❏	❏	❏	❏	❏
4. I understand the expected benefits of the project.	❏	❏	❏	❏	❏
5. I feel that the project will help position us for further success.	❏	❏	❏	❏	❏
6. I support the company's decision to move forward with this project.	❏	❏	❏	❏	❏
7. I am confident that I will be adequately prepared to work in the new environment.	❏	❏	❏	❏	❏
8. I am confident there will be adequate support available after the transition.	❏	❏	❏	❏	❏
9. It is clear to me how this project fits in with other projects under way.	❏	❏	❏	❏	❏
10. I feel the project team is accepting input and addressing feedback from my area	❏	❏	❏	❏	❏

4. What is the number one thing you would like to know about the project?

5. General comments:

Thank you for completing the survey.

Key Element #5: Institute Cohesive Policies and Procedures

As part of your governance process pertaining to policies and procedures, you must plan your timetable accurately, as we touched on earlier. The project's change management person usually reports to the project manager. This structure can certainly work, but it sets up a tension. Let's step back a minute and think about a nine-month-long project. That project will have three major phases:

> **KEEPING IT SMOOTH**
>
> One of the most overlooked challenges in implementing new work instructions involves finding all the places where the old instructions exist. I've seen Standard Operating Procedures, Department Work Instructions, and new employee orientation materials all provide different directions as to how to perform a particular job. If you are issuing new directions, find all the old documentation and get rid of it!

- Organizing
- Designing and building
- Deploying

Executives need to get the project organized and kicked off. The team needs to design what the future state will look like, build the new processes, and create the organizational structure or systems to support that design. Last, the team must roll out the new program into the organization. In rough terms, each of these phases takes up about a third of the project's time.

Unfortunately, project managers tend to build project plans that work like a relay race. Person 1 gets 1.5 minutes to run around the track. So do persons 2 and 3. Person 4 then has 15 seconds to run around the track to win the race. This is a great plan, unless you're person 4. Unfortunately, in a change project as a change leader, you are person 4. And when you write the plan (as opposed to the project manager), you tend to say, "I need 1.5 minutes to run around the track. And this means everybody else gets 45 seconds."

Whoever writes the plan needs to take into account that there is a tension between the first phases and the last phases. Handled incorrectly, change management gets too little time to be successful throughout these phases. Ensure that you have a seat at the table when the decisions are made regarding how much time the change process needs. Push for that voice, or you will wind up with 15 seconds to run around the track.

Your policies should include all the documentation on how to do the job and what to do if it isn't done properly. It includes everything in your process blueprint and also involves management of issues and risks. It illustrates your procedures for getting the job done properly.

Risk Management

Inevitably, every change involves risks. Maybe you've heard the term "stranger danger." Just like a venture into a dark alley to get to a favorite restaurant a block away, even the most positive and productive change project brings some unknowns. The key is to anticipate unknowns and have procedures already in place to deal with them.

WHY SHOULD YOU CARE ABOUT RISK?

You may ask why I'm suggesting that you as the change manager get knee-deep in risk management. This is typically the project manager's responsibility. The reality is, most big change initiatives get into trouble due to people-related issues, and people-related issues are the change manager's responsibility. Issues and risks therefore need to be managed aggressively. Your career will depend on doing so. Insist that a good process is in place.

Part of your governance process should involve creating a formal risk management process. Managing risks will enable team members to:

- Improve the likelihood that they will achieve change objectives on time and on budget.
- Improve the team's understanding of how the project relates to business operations.
- Improve the performance of the project team by ensuring it has a common understanding of change goals and potential weak areas.
- Reduce the impact of the inevitable events that have the potential to negatively impact your progress.

Your risk management plan should contain the following elements:

Identifying. Every member of the project team should have the opportu-

nity and responsibility to identify risks for the rest of the
team. Keep a centralized list of
these risks (creating a simple
Excel file on a shared drive
works fine). Key attributes of
documenting a *risk* are:

> **Risk** A threat that may pre-
> vent the program from
> reaching its stated goals.
> You cannot eliminate risk, **KEY TERM**
> but you can anticipate what might get in
> the way of success and take action to
> ameliorate it.

- What phase of the program the risk is related to
- A description of the risk
- The risk's potential impact
- The probability of the risk creating the impact
- The risk manager
- A description of the mitigation activities required

MANAGING ISSUES LIKE THEY ARE RISKS

TRICKS OF THE TRADE

You can use a similar approach to manage issues. An *issue* is a topic that requires project team attention to resolve. Left unmanaged, an issue might grow into a risk; but at this point, issues merely require attention to resolve. Key attributes of documenting an *issue* are to address the following:

- Title of the issue
- Who the issue is assigned to (the issue owner)
- The issue's priority
- A description of the issue
- What phase of the program the issue relates to
- Whether the issue relates to other issues
- When the issue is due to be resolved

Assessing. Your project manager should assess and rank risks. *Risk ranking* is one way to perform this assessment. It involves a simple weighted calculation that captures the size of the potential impact and the probability the risk will arise.

Potential Impacts. You classify impacts based on their ability to delay the project.

- An impact of 3 (high) indicates a three-month delay or more
- An impact of 2 (medium) indicates a one- to three-month delay in implementation

■ An impact of 1 (low) indicates a one week to one-month delay.

Probability. See probability scoring in the scale described Table 11-1.

Rating	Score	Description
Very Low	20	Highly unlikely to occur; however, still must be monitored as it could grow through the course of the project
Low	40	Unlikely to occur; however, still needs to be monitored as it could grow through the course of the project
Medium	60	Likely to occur
High	80	Very likely to occur based on current information
Very High	100	Presently occurring

Table 11-1. Probability scoring

If you create a system like this for managing and assessing risks, you will be setting up a governance feature that works for you in your change goal.

Key Element #6: Foster a Culture of Collaboration

Early in this chapter, we talked about two distinct culture problems: a sense of entitlement and a reduced sense of accountability. Both lead to glitches or failures in a change plan.

We've talked a fair bit in this chapter about how to set up systems to keep people accountable. We've also discussed governance to clarify roles and responsibilities—preventing an undue sense of entitlement from gaining the traction to develop.

In the next chapter, we take this a step further to address some components of a change process that can interfere with even the best change plan. Specifically, *conflict is inevitable, despite effective governance.* We discuss what it's like to engage in a change process and how you can foster a culture that collaborates through conflict.

For the purposes of this chapter, I'd like you to simply understand that governance helps change projects go well, but culture issues can destroy or cement your change goals. And culture issues all boil down to one thing: a failure of leadership. Governance provides the yin and the yang of your leadership. In the next and final chapter, we discuss how *strength of leadership* combined with *employees' willingness to act* create the formula that assures the success of your change initiative.

Manager's Checklist for Chapter 11

☑ Any organization may struggle with culture or performance issues. As a manager, you need to know how to use governance *to ensure that people do what they need to do.*

☑ There are six elements that guide governance. If you employ these six elements, you will have systems in place to proactively circumvent or address any culture or performance issues you encounter.

☑ One of the most important elements in governance involves making sure your objectives are clearly thought out, defined, and communicated. Once the objectives are clear, you need to define or refer to your guiding principles. Guiding principles are the rules by which your organization will make all future decisions.

☑ To ensure that people properly act on their authority, make sure their roles and responsibilities are clear.

☑ Your policies should include all the documentation on how to do all the project tasks, and what to do if they aren't done properly. The policies include everything in your process blueprint, and also involve management of issues and risks.

☑ Culture issues can destroy or cement your change goals. Culture issues all boil down to one thing: a failure of leadership.

**Chapter
12**

What Is It Really Like to Create Change?

Keep calm and carry on.

—1939 poster, by British Ministry of Information

Implementing a major change initiative is somewhat like pregnancy. When you or your partner first takes the pregnancy test, let's assume you are both elated at the good news. You can't wait to tell your closest friends and relatives. For the next three months, you begin to adjust to the fact that things will never be the same. While you're still excited, nausea and stress begin to cloud the mother's excitement. She becomes apprehensive but is soothed by knowing you still have time to adjust.

By the second trimester, the pregnancy is getting uncomfortable. As the bump grows, so does the inability to sleep. More energy is needed to feed that expanding womb. My wife needed more support than ever, and at this stage it was not only emotional support she needed, but physical support as well.

Next comes the final trimester when many women question whether they can make it to the end. By this time, the reality of having a child can't be avoided; it's literally under their noses. The pregnancy is real and really uncomfortable. Worries about costs and lost income undoubtedly set in.

Then comes birth. There is a lot of drama and pain. And it results in this amazing—and very real—child. That child looks adorable—but also cries all the time, refuses to sleep, and spits up everything it eats. And the

175

SMART

MANAGING

KEEP CALM AND CARRY ON

Let's go back to the quote that opened this chapter, "Keep calm and carry on." This quote was originally printed on a British poster in 1939 to help citizens stay calm even amidst potential pending invasion. It's since been resurrected, and today is an unofficial motto of British nurses—posted in many hospital wards. And it's a quote that will serve you well as a change leader—as it's a reminder to *keep your emotions cool, and your eyes ahead.*

baby expects that you know how to handle these situations and make everything okay.

At first, your baby is unable to do anything for himself. He can't even find his own fists. You wonder if he will ever become fluent enough to function. How can you keep up with all of your normal activities while trying to adjust to the changes and "get" this whole parenting thing?

A change project is similar. You may start with an exciting kickoff where you do a "rah rah" meeting to get the troops energized. You then slowly begin to adjust to the change—realizing there are some scary realities ahead. The change itself is far enough away that you have time to prepare—so you get to work on it at a reasonable pace.

The middle phase starts to get a little uncomfortable. You need energy to sustain the the team members as they grow into their responsibilities and carry them out. Your destination is still at a distance, but it's obviously out there—and you can't avoid worrying about what is to come. You discover that the work of planning and implementing would be much easier if this were your only "day job" instead of an additional responsibility you've taken on.

The phase before go-live is full of discomfort. There is a lot to do and many unknowns, despite how prepared you have tried to be. The change is coming—whether you want it or not.

Go-live is an emotional mix of relief with a sense of accomplishment, excitement, dread, and fear. It's *really* here. Now what? There are these little voices crying and needing your help—in the form of employees adjusting to changed processes, systems, and organization structures. *Will people ever learn to work on their own?* you wonder. Will you ever be able to go back to your "regular" job?

> ### THE LAMAZE METHOD
> **SMART**
>
> The analogy to childbirth can be extended even further. Lamaze is a childbirth technique that provides mothers with an understanding of how to deal with childbirth pain in ways that comfort and ease the birthing process. With that comes confidence. This chapter is **MANAGING** the Lamaze lesson for change management. Remember: focus on the goal and breathe. You can do this—just like so many before you already have.

In this chapter, we discuss what it's like to be in the middle of a change and the mindset you need so your fellow employees will go where the sponsor needs them to go.

Assessing Your Change Environment: The Four Culture Changes

I've given you the change management playbook. But now that you have reached the final chapter, do you know which plays to call? Do you know how to best use the strengths of your team to get the desired result, even in the heat of the moment? Probably not yet, but like a football coach who can feel the game unfold, you can assess your environment and leaders and carve out the appropriate role for yourself.

To have confidence in your role, you need to understand the different types of change environments you will face. Why? Although you may be able to help people change, you may not be able to change their environment. There are differences in organizational culture and leadership that create opportunities for and limitations on what you can do as a change manager. You need to know how people operate, how leaders think, and how to work with those factors.

> ### GET NUANCED
> **CAUTION**
>
> In the *Psychology of Science* (Maurice Bassett Publishing, 1966), psychologist Abraham Maslow first wrote a dictum called Maslow's Hammer that states, "If all you have is a hammer, everything looks like a nail." I don't want you to see every problem as a nail, and I don't want you swinging around a hammer. As a change manager, I want you to "get nuanced" enough that you can see different types of change environments and adjust your support style accordingly. By this, I mean I want you to assess the subtle differences among people and environments and adjust to best suit your organization's change initiative.

SMART

HERDING CATS

MANAGING

Ever try to herd cats? Go ahead and try to slap leashes on them and pull them to your destination. They'll freak out, escape, and go running for the hills—or scratch you to bits. Nor can you give the cats a speech about the direction you want them to go, and then go take a nap while you expect them to heed your instructions. No, you have to know how to motivate the cats on their terms to do what you want. Provide enough catnip along the way that they aren't trying to escape. And at times, that might mean picking them up and delivering them safely to the desired destination.

To keep calm and carry on through your change, balance *the strength of your leadership team* with a *willingness among your employees to act*. Where is your organization when it comes to balancing these two? Take a look at Figure 12-1. How you act depends on which quadrant you fall into.

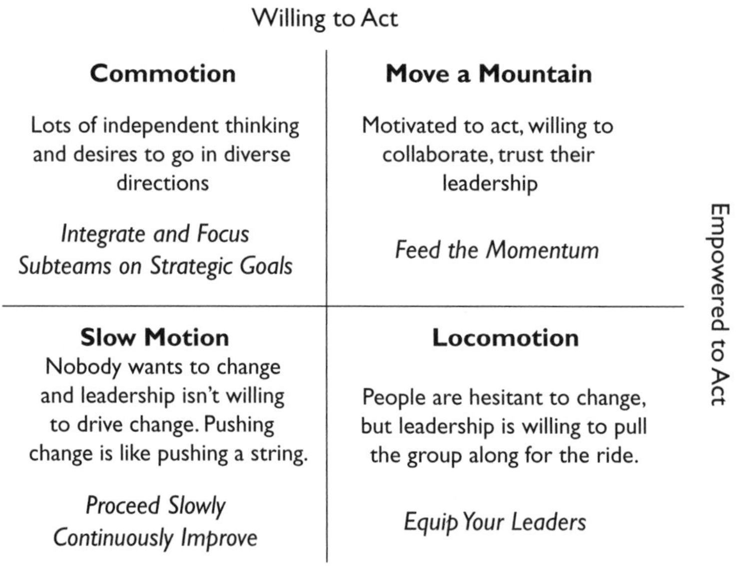

Willing to Act

Commotion	**Move a Mountain**
Lots of independent thinking and desires to go in diverse directions	Motivated to act, willing to collaborate, trust their leadership
Integrate and Focus Subteams on Strategic Goals	*Feed the Momentum*
Slow Motion	**Locomotion**
Nobody wants to change and leadership isn't willing to drive change. Pushing change is like pushing a string.	People are hesitant to change, but leadership is willing to pull the group along for the ride.
Proceed Slowly Continuously Improve	*Equip Your Leaders*

Empowered to Act

Figure 12-1. The culture of a change initiative

Move to Maintain. If your culture falls in the Move a Mountain quadrant, people are motivated to act, trust their leadership, and are ready for action. In this case, your job is to feed the momentum that will build naturally. You provide support as management, and employees figure it all out on their own.

Locomotion. If your culture falls on the Locomotion quadrant, your organization has strong leaders, but employees are unwilling to act. Leaders are likely tugging at them like cats on a leash. If this is your environment, you'll need to equip leaders to engage in the change. Your job won't be small; it will be big. Your sponsor will be pulling a large train— and some of the cars may not even be on the tracks. He or she will need lots of help.

Commotion. If your culture falls in the Commotion quadrant, you experience people with a high willingness to act, but no strength of leadership. Players make decisions without guidance, likely running amuck. If this is your culture, your sponsor won't be focusing on integrating the work of all the different change participants. For the organization to be successful, you'll need to step in and keep the subteams focused on integrating their work products with each other. If you don't do this, the result will appear to be built by a committee, and your organization might be worse off than it was originally. You have a big job.

Slow Motion. If your culture falls in the Slow Motion quadrant, you neither have strong leadership nor people who are willing to act. If you experience this, your organization will need to proceed slowly to get both leaders and employees on board. Your job is to avoid the mistake of aspiring too high.

So now that you can look at a change situation and have a feel for your general tone in creating change, let's take a look at the personal characteristics you need to employ during your change. It is these personal characteristics that people will be taking their cues from.

DEVELOP A WINNING "CHANGE ATTITUDE"

TRICKS OF THE TRADE

In the May 30, 2008, edition of *The Wall Street Journal*, an article appeared on Campbell's Soup Company and innovation. A callout box provided five tips on leading a transformation from their CEO, Douglas Conant. Here is what was suggested:

1. Bring an "all things are possible" attitude to the work.
2. Confront the brutal facts and be clear-eyed about the situation.
3. Set high standards and make expectations clear, as the ability to mobilize people is the key to success.
4. Give the organization time to do things right.
5. Do what you say you will; this is about performance, not intentions.

The Characteristics You Need

As a manager directing a team through change, your job will be easier if you demonstrate several competencies:

- Conflict management
- Compassion
- Composure
- Listening
- Motivation of others
- Patience
- Standing alone

We focus on *conflict management* and *compassion* and sum up all the attributes suggested by the word *stewardship*. (For excellent insight into workplace competencies, read the works of Robert W. Eichinger and Michael M. Lombardo for Lominger Limited, Inc.)

SMART MANAGING

REASSURE

These cues are important. Early in my career, I worked in a company that got a new CEO. Within the next three months, many members of the HR department began to leave. I was informed by an experienced cynic that this was a bad sign, "People in human resources don't like dealing with bad things, so bad things are coming." Sure enough, they came.

Your ability to stand up and convincingly say, "Everything is going to be okay," will help things actually turn out okay.

Handling Conflict: Seek Collaboration Not Consensus

How do you avoid conflict and create agreement?

When there are only a couple of people involved in a project, decision-making protocols aren't a worry. Having a larger group, however, complicates matters. Some people may want to vote on topics. Some may want to defer to the leader. Some may want consensus. Frankly, there is no correct answer for every situation. There is, however, a universal truth to share about using consensus in a change—that is, *consensus is not the goal.*

In reality, consensus frequently means "the minimum that we can all agree to." In other words, you will not reach an aspirational goal if you

Managing Inertia and Velocity

Think about Sir Isaac Newton and his work on mechanics. Every high school student learns about inertia: "An object in motion tends to stay in motion. An object at rest tends to stay at rest." The teen remembers this concept as a justification to stay on the couch. The parent, on the other hand, is well aware of Newton's first law of motion: "The velocity of a body remains constant unless the body is acted upon by an external force." The parent typically provides that force.

Organizations are no different. They require an external force to change direction. That external force is pushing on something that doesn't want to move. That resistance plays out as conflict.

operate by consensus. You need to understand that conflict will come, and your job will be to lead through that conflict.

A successful change initiative does not come about through attaining the minimum that the whole team can agree to. Change requires moving out of a comfort zone and going to a new place. People will disagree. Discomfort is inevitable. Instead of instituting policies of "You must accept this lowest common denominator" or "You must accept this dictator's 'consensus of one,'" collaboration involves people in the process so that they feel like owners in the decision making. The key is to anticipate the discomfort and take steps to keep participation alive despite it.

Think of Your Teenager

Leading change is similar to parenting a teenager. You see a lot of progress but also many challenges. Part of becoming an adult involves rebelling against adults. Rebelling is how teens develop an understanding of who they are. A teenager's rebellion is both a necessary part of the development process and a source of frustration to the parent. If you're a parent of a teen, you know that calmness is a powerful force.

Calmness during change is just as powerful. As a change leader or manager, know that you will need patience and calmness. All the negativity and pushback you will hear during your project is part of the growth process.

Be prepared to deal with disagreement with these three tips:

1. **Set boundaries.** State right up front that the group will not be ruled by consensus. Consensus will mean that you fall short of your goals. You can ask for feedback and input at appropriate times, as I stated earlier;

CONFLICT AVOIDANCE: WHY "MIDWEST NICE" DOESN'T ALWAYS WORK

CAUTION I'm originally from New York, but I now live in the Midwest. By reputation, Midwesterners are *nice*—which seems like a good thing, right? The part that might not be so good is that Mid-westerners are also known for avoiding conflict. The stereotype suggests that they would rather put on a happy face than tell the blunt truth about what they think of the neighbor's awful new picket fence.

The problem with being "Midwest nice" is that it can often become passive-aggressive. Passive aggression involves addressing a problem by *not doing something*, or by doing something aggressive in a nonassertive, passive, indirect way. Passive aggression is often comprised of resistance and negative attitudes.

If you have a problem, addressing it indirectly can make things worse. Be nice, but not "Midwest nice." Effective managers foster collaboration without going to all lengths to avoid confrontations. Embrace conflict as a positive thing; with it comes the means to drive better collaboration. Find ways to work through conflict, but don't pretend it doesn't exist or create extra drama by not dealing with it effectively.

but be clear about when it will *not* be incorporated, and which aspects of the change initiative are *not* up for reevaluation or critique.

2. **Be ready for conflict.** Brace yourself for disagreement and conflict. A change management practitioner who avoids conflict will not be successful. Disagreement is part of the process of getting to a new place. Eliminate denial, and focus on accepting and moving through the conflict.

3. **Realize it isn't personal.** Remember the change curve? The sometimes-intense emotions are normal. Expect them. Realize they are not a result of a failure on your part. They are inevitable. Even if people get heated and seem to blame you, try to insulate yourself from taking their words personally. And in the process, try to detach from making your reactions toward them personal.

LET EMOTIONS SETTLE

Take a break if you need to to let emotions settle. Remember the change goals, and ask yourself whether any response or reaction will help or hurt that outcome. Focus your responses on meeting those goals, not on getting even with whatever might have been said.

Implement "Cumulative Voting" as a Means of Collaboration

Cumulative voting can speed decision making in a large group setting while also fostering participation and collaboration. The process I use and recommend in many cases involves lots of sticky notes, adhesive sticker dots, and a structured process. Let's use an example of a large group that needs to decide how they will allocate resources. They initially disagree about which resources should be allocated first, and this indecision paralyzes to their efforts. Here is a five-step process for using cumulative voting to foster participation in such times of conflict (Note: Use this also before conflict arises!):

Define the topics to be discussed. Develop a potential structure for organizing your business problems or questions. I have used the 10 topics from the Organizational Alignment Model in Chapter 4 on several occasions for this purpose, but any structure can work. As a refresher, the 10 topics are: objectives, culture, strategies, processes, systems, controls, structure, people, rewards, and change leadership.

Discuss and gather input. Ask the group to discuss one category of problem or topic at a time. There are no "bad" answers or concepts in this process. Encourage the group to listen as their coworkers discuss the change project and to capture the topics they are hearing on the sticky notes. Encourage them to add their own topics, even in categories you haven't introduced.

Display and group the topics. Instruct the group to put all the sticky notes on the wall. While the group is discussing the next category, somebody can group like items. Repeat this process until you've gone through all your categories and assigned each set of notes to a category.

Vote on priorities. Distribute an equal number of sticker dots to each participant. Ask each group member to place the dots where he or she would like to allocate resources. People can place their dots as they see fit. Some people will spread their dots around. Some people will bunch their dots around their personal priorities.

Tally the votes. Tally the resulting dot display for a decision, with the items receiving the most dots becoming the key priorities to address. This involves input from each group member, with a clear means of achieving an action-oriented result—hence the term *cumulative voting*.

This approach uses collective wisdom, participation, and a non-judgmental process to reach a decision—while hearing everyone's voice.

Work Through Resistance

Resistance takes many forms. Employees may show obvious signs of resistance, as when they strongly object or refuse to cooperate with the change. Sometimes resistance takes on a more subtle aspect, as when employees show apathy or have difficulty concentrating on what they are being told or taught concerning the change.

CAUTION

QUIET DOESN'T ALWAYS MEAN CALM

I had a client who trained as an EMT in Germany. He was taught that when you come upon an accident scene, you should initially ignore the people who are screaming. They will be fine. Go to the people who are quiet. They're the ones who need your help.

Similarly in the change process, don't ignore the quiet people and focus all your attention on those who are screaming with drama. The quiet people may also be struggling, but may lack the tools or demeanor to scream about it. Check in with people regularly to ensure they are okay. Take the pulse of every employee—not only those who are making the most noise.

It's vital that you, as a change manager, not only anticipate resistance but have a plan to detect, diagnose, and eradicate it. Your job is to support the sponsor in overcoming this resistance. You must understand why employees resist change so that, from the beginning of your initiative, you can undertake preventive measures to minimize its potential effect on your effort's success.

TRICKS OF THE TRADE

DEAL WITH IT

The sponsor or line managers are the best people to deal with resistance. People who are resisting change don't want to hear from a staff person.

To work through resistance, follow this Three P approach, which we explore next:

- Understand its **Purpose**
- Work through the **Prerequisites**
- Overcome it with **Process**

Purpose. Broadly defined, resistance is a fearful response to change. It's also a natural and predictable phenomenon for a process or environment undergoing change. Sources of resistance are not always clear. As someone supporting the change sponsor, however, you must try to find why employees are resistant to your initiative because, inasmuch as resistance is expected to some extent, it can be a major deterrent to the effort's success. Detection and diagnosis of change resistance, however, is often more difficult than dealing with it once it is fully known.

Prerequisites. To overcome resistance to change, you must determine what precisely is being resisted. In general, there are three fundamental issues—and eight layers of potential change resistance—which can be described as follows:

1. Resistance to *what* to change:
   - "We think the real problem is something else."
   - "The problem is beyond our control, so why are we here?"

2. Resistance on what to change t*o*:
   - "We have a different direction for the solution."
   - "The solution is insufficient."
   - "This solution has a downside to it."

3. Resistance on *how* to change:
   - "This solution cannot be implemented."
   - "We don't know how to implement this solution."
   - "We're afraid to make the change."

Engage employees in a conversation based on this understanding of why they resist. Avoid asking yes/no questions and listen intently to employees as they express their beliefs and feelings. When you hear an unspoken "but," you've discovered where their concern lies.

SEE BEYOND FACE VALUE

Occasionally, you may hear employees voice objections at a seemingly higher level of resistance by saying, "This just isn't doable," but their concerns are actually at a lower level. They may accept the case for change but see the solution as flawed.
Do not accept their words of objection at face value; ask questions to dig deeper and understand more clearly the reasons for their dissent.

While engaging in a conversation with employees to overcome resistance, ascertain:

- Whether you and the employees agree on what the problem is
- Whether you and the employees agree on what to change to
- Whether you and the employees agree on how to make the change

The probability of a successful transformation is greater if each of the employee's answers to those questions are "yes." If not, you now know where your major challenge lies in achieving employee commitment to your change effort.

As you strive to eliminate their concern, focus employees' attention on how they will benefit from the change. Without painting an overly rosy picture, communicate how the initiative will provide advantages in terms of:

- Increased security
- Stronger personal relationships and contacts
- More money
- Less time and effort
- Enhanced authority
- Improved status or prestige
- Better working conditions
- Greater self-satisfaction

Further, you may wish to explain how the change effort will result in a new professional challenge, provide opportunity to set the course for future progress, and/or create new customer bases and revenue streams, if appropriate.

Process. The root causes of resistance are fairly predictable, but there are good responses to each type of resistance, as shown in Table 12-1.

As Table 12-1 shows, employees may have multiple reasons for resisting change. In addition, they may anticipate a loss of something they value, which can include any of the following:

- Security
- Friends and acquaintances
- Money
- Pride and satisfaction
- Responsibility

Root Causes of Resistance	How a Change Leader Should Respond
Belief that the risk of changing is greater than the risk of maintaining the status quo.	In making the case for change, you must deal with risk perceptions head-on. You may wish to use numbers to advocate on behalf of change; numbers allow you to engage the rational minds of your employees, who then stand a better chance of emotionally connecting with your initiative.
A negative attitude toward the organization—even before the change initiative commences—and resentfulness or bitterness toward your effort.	Devote your time and energy in helping them to see the positive aspects of the change, but do not sugarcoat the possibilities or give them false hopes.
The perception that the change involves too much work and confusion for too little benefit.	Less rhetoric and more demonstration can make a huge difference in helping people to envision how they will work in the future. Take advantage of pilot programs to make the change real for those impacted. Help them understand that sacrifices in the short term will be worth a more advantageous future.
Objections to the method by which change is being implemented within the organization. This is apt to be a strongly held concern if employees do not believe they are being given adequate opportunity to participate in the transformation.	To avoid this prospect, involve employees early and often in the change process.
Employees may fear they do not have the skills necessary to adapt to the change effectively.	In some cases, their fears are unwarranted, and your ability to motivate them will help them come to terms with the change. In other cases, they indeed lack the necessary skills. Make sure you place priority on training programs.

Table 12-1. Root causes of change resistance and responses (continued on next page)

Root Causes of Resistance	How a Change Leader Should Respond
Employees may feel overwhelmed by change and fatigued as a result.	Motivate and encourage employees, praise their accomplishments, practice patience, and allow employees to vent their emotions if and when appropriate.
Employees may be revealing a healthy skepticism in making sure the ideas behind the change are solid. They may want to vet the ideas to ensure success.	Listen to skeptics; their questions, concerns, and suggestions may add great value.
Suspicions about a hidden agenda.	Demonstrate your good faith and sincere interest in the success of the business while keeping communications open and direct with impacted employees.
A proposed change may threaten self-identity. For example, when factory workers discover the change requires that they do less with their hands and more through automated equipment, they may fear losing their identity as craftspeople. Consequently, they believe the intrinsic rewards that lured them to a certain line of work will be lost through change.	In some cases, the assessment may be correct. The only answer is to help employees to understand and desire the rewards that will come with the change and to realize how their self-worth will be enhanced in the future.

Table 12-1. Root causes of change resistance and responses (continued)

- Authority
- Status
- Professional and/or personal success
- Chances for advancement

Often change seems to reshuffle the fortunes of employees, with some standing to gain and others appearing to lose. Those in the latter camp will likely be allied against the change because they feel it is contrary to their best interests, and rightly so. While you can undertake strategies to mitigate their opposition, you are obligated to present the inevitability of the change given the risk landscape and help employees cope. The reality is that, in most change programs, some employees will choose to leave the organization. In some instances, that is for the best.

The Dos and Don'ts of Compassion

We all feel warm and fuzzy when people show they care about us personally, but what about in the workplace? Some managers are biased against applying compassion in the workplace. Why? Many managers are *unsure how to handle strong emotions in others while still retaining a professional distance.*

As a manager, it might make you uncomfortable to think about opening the door to such emotions. Get over it, and quickly. Strong change leaders know it's imperative to show compassion, especially during times of change. Compassion shows that you empathize with your team members. From a place of empathy, you calm the rough seas of conflict.

Compassion starts by accepting people as they are. Refer to the change curve in Figure 2-1. Remember the emotions your people are experiencing: denial, anger, sadness, bargaining, acceptance, and so forth.

Handling people with compassion will open to the door to many of the other skills necessary in handling change.

OFFERING COMPASSION

TRICKS OF THE TRADE

Here are tips for offering compassion:

- Put yourself in that person's shoes. How would you feel and what would you want? Express empathy.
- Realize that compassion may involve mere listening. You don't have to offer advice to be effective, nor do you have to provide counseling. Some of the best psychiatric counselors listen for more than 80 percent of their session time with clients. Why? Listening without judgment, critique, or interruption offers more compassion than most people ever receive. Be that kind of listener.
- Don't prejudge the person or situation.
- If the situation involves more than you can handle at work, invite the employee to meet with a professional outside of work hours to discuss it.

COMPASSIONATE CUTTING

CAUTION

You may find yourself on a project where people are going to lose their jobs. They may be your friends or parents of your children's friends. It will be very hard. But you need to keep one thing in mind: it is necessary to leave the company for the rest of the people in the company to succeed. Management has made a decision that the long-term success of the business relies on investing in something new and disinvesting in something old. It is hard to think of your friend as a "disinvestment," but you need to think of the investment in your other friends. It is very hard, but the people who are staying are counting on you to make the decisions necessary to ensure that they will continue to be employed.

BE EMPATHETIC, NOT SYMPATHETIC

Empathy involves understanding employees' emotions so you can relate to them as you help them. Sympathy involves feeling sorry for employees. Empathy fosters forward movement. Sympathy keeps people stuck. Use empathy, not sympathy, as you lead people through tough times.

Wrapping It Up: Your Job as a Change Manager

Let's get back to the task at hand: your job as a change manager. I hope after reading this book, you have a clearer idea of what goes into managing a big change. To illustrate the confusion around this role, I'd like to share a story.

Last week was a busy week. We began work with a new client, and I was battling a minidepression over an assessment that my profession might add no value to society.

My battle started with an article I read about Wall Street wizards, hedge funds, and derivatives. The author, an Andy Rooney type, claimed if a person couldn't explain what he or she did for a living in two sentences, he or she wasn't adding any value to society. Farmers, doctors, plumbers, and janitors were all on the good list. "Liquidity tranche default analysts" were definitely on the bad list.

So, I thought, if I can't define "organizational change management consultant" in two sentences, does this mean I am not adding value to society? Does my mother-in-law have any idea what I do when I say I

FIRE CAREFULLY   SMART

I just got a phone call from somebody who needed to cancel a meeting we had scheduled for next week. It seems a few days ago, he and most of his department were precipitously let go. He walked out the door without a badge or laptop but still holding **MANAGING** his BlackBerry—loaded with e-mails, contacts, etc. Two days later, the Black-Berry's data has not been wiped. He used that information to cancel appointments that had been set up but that nobody from his old employer intended to keep. He also used that information to network a bit for his own benefit.

Needless to say, his previous employer's equity took a hit in my opinion, and I doubt we will be doing business with that firm in the future. He, on the other hand, did me a favor by respecting my time so I don't show up for a meeting that isn't going to happen. I'm inclined to repay the favor.

The winners and losers in this conversation could have been reversed if the employer had a workforce reduction plan that respected its people, customers, and suppliers. It isn't hard; it just takes effort. Let's put aside whether they were cutting "fat" or "muscle." They cut at least one of their opportunities for future growth.

Think about it if you are doing the cutting. You have the opportunity to fire with compassion and careful planning—or the chance to create even more conflict.

"help clients' managers lead their people quickly through organizational changes. I help by being a project manager, strategist, writer, teacher, coach, scorecard keeper, presenter, analyst, tactician, assessor, trainer, and graphic artist."

The answer is no. Those two sentences, although accurate, really don't get the meaning across. I'm afraid I have failed the author's test. I need more than two sentences.

As a manager during change, maybe you feel the same. What's your role? What does this change really mean? How do you define all of this in two sentences?

If unbound by the two-sentence constraint, I might frame a conversation about the work to be done with questions about an organization's relative potential for success in this way:

- Does it have the right goals and plans? Will the plans enable the organization to reach the goals?
- Do people understand what they are to do? Great plans that aren't understood have no value. How does the leader ensure that people

understand the plan? Are they organized to succeed, and do they have all the enablers necessary to achieve the goals?

■ How engaged are people to achieve the goals and work the plans? The right plans, even if well understood, will not be successful if people don't want to make the necessary effort.

Depending on the answers, your job changes greatly. At the most general, your job is to help the organization answer yes to all these questions. The specific work changes based on the nature of the challenge, the scope of services being provided, and the tactics required.

Regardless of my perspective on whether certain jobs add value to society, there is value to an organization in moving past change and returning to its mission. The faster the move, the more value is created. If you can speed that move, you help create value.

As an aside, I decided on Sunday—which just happened to be Father's Day—that the author was wrong. Sometimes more than two sentences are needed. To prove the point—try defining "father" in two sentences. Or—obviously—"mother."

This may get you thinking about what your role is.

Model Stewardship

Regardless of how you define your job as a change manager, I like to think of that role as a steward. I'd like to think you can answer the question, "What do you do?" by saying:

■ I help leaders move their teams through challenging times.

■ I help by taking the leader's goal as my own and influencing the team toward achieving that goal.

The concept of taking care of something that doesn't belong to you and leading by only influencing (and no authority) is the heart of stewardship. I feel that no definition of change leader, or effective manager, would be complete without a discussion of stewardship. In fact, stewardship is such a powerful and meaningful concept to me that I have chosen to end this book with a discussion of the concept.

Why are stewards so important? Stewards are responsible for ensuring that things are managed and run smoothly. Stewards are expected to deliver a result for the leader even if they don't own the resources to get things done. You have probably heard calls from environmental groups to become "stewards of the Earth." Even though you don't own the oceans, for example, they remind you that you may be able to affect the oceans by cleaning a local stream or by composting.

Similarly, the leader of your organization "owns" the responsibility for the people in that organization. You are there helping to move this organization through change, taking care of the employees

> **FAMILY REUNION**   SMART
>
> Think about planning your family reunion. If you assign roles for each person, you create stewards—leaders who lack **MANAGING** formal authority but are empowered to act. Change management is similarly all about stewardship—taking care of that which does not belong to you.

as if they were your own. The change activities that occur during the various stages help move people into awareness, understanding, and participation—delivering a change that is both powerful and sustainable.

The steward accepts responsibility for the performance of the organization—advocating for it as needed. The steward is committed to the project until completion and is willing to advocate strongly for the organization and its leader.

Stewards, like change champions, must be able to influence others even if they don't control the day-to-day change project. This can be challenging, not only because

> **Steward** Someone who takes on the role of overseeing something that he or she does not actually **KEY TERM** own or control.

employees must be able to trust and provide key information to this steward, but also because the steward must stay committed to the change even when he or she doesn't control the details.

How, then, do you foster stewardship? Start by modeling it. Take responsibility for your key areas—even those you may not control. Show interest in what others are doing. Be available to offer support to team members.

Then, pay it forward. Assign stewardship roles based on employees' skill levels. Reward them for a job well done by shifting less crucial or rewarding work to someone else in the organization. Let them shine, and take pride in their work.

To build a team that keeps calm and carries on, empower people. Show them how to be company owners—by showing them areas where they can hold responsibility and thrive. Give them not only a clear vision on where the organization is going but a clear idea of how they fit in—today and tomorrow. In the process, you may foster an environment of people who can so readily adapt to the nuanced needs of the organization that they become tomorrow's change leaders—driving the company ahead through the decades.

And now, I leave you to the task of herding cats, playing football, or delivering babies. Whatever your organization's goal, you are equipped to move into your change while leading others through it. In the process of reading this book, I hope you found useful tools as well as inspiration. I'd love to hear from you on how it's going. Drop me a line, as you ASPIRE to move ahead!

> *We should all be concerned about the future because we will have to spend the rest of our lives there.*
> —Charles F. Kettering

Manager's Checklist for Chapter 12

- ☑ To successfully change, assess where your change initiative culture lies, and make adaptations to strengthen leadership and employees' willingness to act.

- ☑ Conflict is inevitable and is a part of any change initiative.

- ☑ Don't be passive-aggressive in an attempt to avoid confrontation. Be direct and honest, and keep your emotions calm. Show empathy, not sympathy.

- ☑ Your goal should be to foster collaboration, not consensus.

- ☑ Compassion starts with empathy and is something all managers should get good at.

- ☑ Your goal should be to model stewardship, that is, responsibility for something you do not own.

Index

About the Author

Stephen Rock is the founder of The Brookside Group, a Kansas City-based organizational change management consulting firm. The Brookside Group works with its clients to help them become faster and more agile organizations by moving internal stakeholders swiftly through major change initiatives.

For more than 20 years, Stephen has worked on corporate reorganizations, enterprise resource planning implementations, major business process reengineering efforts, rapid growth ramp-ups, and culture change initiatives. He has worked with the human resources, information technology, communication, finance, and sales functions at many of the Fortune 100 companies. Stephen speaks on leading change initiatives at a number of industry conferences.

Stephen holds a degree in Economics from Colgate University and resides in Kansas City, Missouri. Stephen would be happy to discuss the challenges you might be facing and can be reached at stephen.rock@the brooksidegroup.com. You can learn more about The Brookside Group at www.thebrooksidegroup.com.